The Messy Bible: Judges

Everyone Did What Was Right in Their Own Eyes

Introduction: Nobody Wants to Follow the Rules

The first volume of this series was about a book full of bad examples.

This volume is about what happens when an entire nation decides to become one.

Genesis documented the problem at the level of individuals. Adam and Eve took what was not theirs. Cain killed his brother and lied about it. Abraham lied about his wife — twice, to two different rulers, for the same reason, with the same result. Jacob stole. Judah exploited. The patriarchs, one after another, operated on the same fundamental premise: I will decide what is good and evil. I will determine what I am owed. I will do what is right in my own eyes.

Judges is what it looks like when that premise scales up.

The Laws Existed. Nobody Followed Them.

This is important to establish before we enter the book. By the time the Israelites cross into Canaan, the law is not a secret. It has been given at Sinai, explained in Leviticus and Numbers, and recited again in its entirety in Deuteronomy — a book whose entire purpose is to remind a community, before they enter a new era, of exactly what they have been asked to do and exactly what will happen if they don't.

Deuteronomy is not subtle. Chapters 27 and 28 lay out the blessings for obedience and the curses for abandonment in language so specific that reading Judges afterward feels less like history and more like watching a prophecy fulfill itself in real time. If you do not follow these commands, your enemies will oppress you. If you serve other gods, you will be handed over to those who hate you. If you abandon the covenant, the framework that holds your community together will dissolve — and the dissolution will accelerate.

Judges is the fulfillment of that warning. Not as divine vindictiveness. As consequence.

The book opens with a list of failures. Tribe after tribe attempts to complete the conquest and settles, instead, for accommodation. The Canaanites are not expelled — they are put to forced labor. They are allowed to remain. The explicit prohibition of Deuteronomy 7 — make no covenant with them, do not intermarry, break down their altars — is not followed. The tribes decide that the prohibited peoples are more useful as laborers than as expelled enemies. The short-term calculation is obvious. The long-term consequences are the rest of the book.

The Angel of the LORD appears at Bokim to deliver what amounts to a legal indictment: you did not obey my voice. The people weep. And then, without repentance, the narrator moves directly to the next cycle.

That pattern — hear the indictment, weep, change nothing — is the pattern of the entire book.

How Quickly Things Go South

The narrator of Judges is unusually explicit about what is happening. Early in chapter two, before a single judge narrative begins, the structure is laid out in plain terms: Israel abandons God. God withdraws protection. An enemy oppresses Israel. Israel cries out. God raises a judge. The judge

delivers. There is rest. The judge dies. Israel immediately —
the text uses that word — abandons God again, more
thoroughly than before.

"More corrupt than their fathers." That phrase appears at
Judges 2:19, and it is the key to reading everything that
follows. The cycle does not level off. It descends. Each iteration
reaches a new floor. The judges grow more morally
compromised. The deliverances grow more ambiguous. The
community that benefits from each rescue does not become
more faithful — it becomes less so. And the book's structure
reflects this: the Othniel episode is eight clean verses; the
Samson narrative runs four chapters and ends in wreckage.

This is not a book about spiritual forgetfulness that God
patiently corrects. It is a book about what happens when a
community is given a framework for flourishing, decides not
to use it, discovers what life looks like without it, and then —
even after being rescued — decides not to use it again.

The laws the community was given were not arbitrary. They
were specific. They prohibited the exploitation of the
vulnerable. They protected the widow, the orphan, the
resident alien. They established judicial accountability,
limited the accumulation of power, and created a framework
within which no single person — and no single tribe — could
operate without reference to something beyond their own
judgment. The law was the binding element. Without it, what
remained was exactly what Judges documents: everyone doing
what was right in their own eyes.

That phrase — "everyone did what was right in their own
eyes" — appears four times in the book. It is the closing
refrain. It is not presented as a neutral description of human
freedom. It is presented as a diagnosis of collapse. In Genesis,

Adam and Eve took for themselves the right to determine good and evil. In Judges, an entire nation operates on that same premise — and the book shows, chapter by chapter, what it produces.

What This Book Does

This volume uses the same three tools established in the Genesis volume.

First: reading each narrative against its downstream legislation. The laws of the Torah are not abstract moral pronouncements. They are reactive documents — they exist because the narratives have already demonstrated, story by story, what happens when humans operate without them. In Judges, the relationship runs in both directions: the law explains what the narrative is violating, and the narrative shows what the law was designed to prevent.

Second: cross-canonical corroboration. Where Judges establishes a pattern, the prophets name it, Jesus engages it, and the epistles close the argument. Paul's spiral in Romans 1 — suppressing the knowledge of God leading to increasing moral darkness — is the New Testament parallel to the Judges cycle. When all three streams point the same direction, the interpretation has earned some confidence.

Third: reading what the text actually says, rather than the version handed down in children's summaries. The children's version of Judges presents Gideon as a hero of faith, Samson as a strongman with one fatal weakness, and Jephthah as a man who made a rash vow. The text presents something considerably darker. Each of these chapters begins with the

version most of us received and then reads the actual text —
at the speed it was written for.

Judges requires a fourth tool: reading the descending arc.
Unlike Genesis, which documents individual failures one story
at a time, Judges is structurally committed to getting worse.
The book is not a collection of independent episodes with a
shared theme. It is a designed collapse. Understanding that
design is the only way to read any single story correctly.

Where It Ends

The book of Judges ends with an unnamed woman's hands on
a threshold in the dark, and a community so morally dissolved
that its response to her death will produce further massacres
and further abductions, compounding the violence rather than
resolving it.

It ends there not because the narrator lost the plot, but
because that is where the logic of the book was always
pointing. A community that will not be governed by a
framework beyond its own judgment — that treats the laws
designed to protect the vulnerable as optional, that
accommodates what it was told to displace, that cycles through
remorse without repentance — eventually becomes the thing
it was supposed to oppose. By the final chapter of Judges, an
Israelite city is doing what Sodom did. The reader who
remembers Genesis 19 is meant to feel the full weight of that.

The refrain that closes the book is not a solution. It is a
diagnosis: "In those days there was no king in Israel. Everyone
did what was right in their own eyes." The absence of a binding
framework is the problem. What should fill that absence —
and whether any institution actually can — is the question the

rest of the canon spends the next several books trying to
answer.

*The laws were given. Nobody followed them. Here is what that
looked like.*

Chapter One: Conquest Incomplete

Reference: Judges 1:1–2:5

The Story We Tell Children

After Joshua died, the tribes of Israel fought to take the land God had promised them. They had some victories and some setbacks. God rebuked them for not finishing the job.

That's the version. It turns the opening of Judges into a logistics problem with a moral lesson attached. The text is doing something far more unsettling.

The Slower Reading

1. The Canaanites Are Not Gone

Judges 1 is a list of failures. Tribe after tribe attempts to drive out the inhabitants of Canaan — and tribe after tribe settles for accommodation instead. The Canaanites are put to forced labor (1:28), not expelled. They dwell alongside Israel (1:29, 30, 33). The text is cataloguing precisely what the Deuteronomic law prohibited — and what Joshua's narrative had presented as essentially accomplished. The tension between Joshua's triumphalism and Judges' inventory of what was actually left undone is not accidental. It is editorial. The book opens by reading against its predecessor.

Deuteronomy 7:2–4 — You shall make no covenant with them, nor show mercy to them. Neither shall you make marriages with them... for they will turn away your sons from following me, that they may serve other gods.

The law was explicit. The failure is documented. The consequences — catalogued across the next eighteen chapters — are presented as the direct result of a choice the tribes made in chapter one.

2. The Angel's Rebuke at Bokim

The Angel of the LORD appears at Bokim to deliver what amounts to a legal indictment: *"I will never break my covenant with you, and you shall make no covenant with the inhabitants of this land; you shall break down their altars. But you have not obeyed my voice."* The people weep — hence Bokim, "weeping" — but no repentance follows. The narrator moves directly to the next cycle.

Judges 2:2–3 — You shall make no covenant with the inhabitants of this land; you shall throw down their altars. But you have not obeyed my voice. Why have you done this? Therefore I also said, I will not drive them out from before you; but they shall be as thorns in your sides, and their gods shall be a snare to you.

This is the structural hinge of the entire book. Every subsequent oppression, every judge narrative, every spiral of apostasy — all of it flows directly from this moment of incomplete obedience in chapter one. The book's argument is already complete on page two. The next nineteen chapters are the evidence.

3. The Tension with Joshua

The opening verses of Judges 1 raise a question the text never directly answers: how do we reconcile the sweeping victories described in Joshua with the litany of failures catalogued here? Scholars have offered various explanations — different sources, different tribal memories, a deliberate editorial juxtaposition. What matters theologically is that the Judges narrator chose to open the book with this inventory. The reader is meant to feel the dissonance. Victory was possible. This is what was chosen instead.

Legal-Canonical Framework

- **Deuteronomy 7:1–5** — explicit prohibition against covenants with Canaanite peoples and their gods

- **Deuteronomy 12:2–3** — command to destroy altars and sacred sites, not accommodate them

- **Numbers 33:55** — explicit warning that those left in the land "shall be as pricks in your eyes and thorns in your sides"

New Testament Resonance

The New Testament does not directly engage the conquest narratives, but the pattern of incomplete obedience — settling for less than the full transformation God calls for, accommodating the thing that is supposed to be displaced — runs throughout Paul's letters and the epistles. Hebrews 12:1 addresses the "sin that so easily entangles" as something requiring active, sustained resistance, not accommodation. The Judges prologue is the Old Testament narrative template for what happens when the entanglement is chosen instead.

Discussion Questions

1. Judges 1 opens by reading against Joshua — presenting the same territory as unconquered that Joshua had declared won. What does it do to your reading of Scripture to find it deliberately correcting itself? What does that suggest about how the canon expects to be read?

2. Each tribe made a practical decision: these Canaanites can be useful as forced laborers. The short-term pragmatism is obvious. Where do you see the same calculation — keeping around what should be displaced because it's currently useful — operating in communities of faith today?

3. The people wept at Bokim. They heard the indictment. They cried. And then nothing changed. What is the difference between remorse and repentance? What would actual repentance have looked like in chapter two?

4. The nations left in the land are described as both a test and a snare (2:22, 3:4). What does it mean for difficulty or temptation to serve a pedagogical function — and does that framing risk becoming an excuse for tolerating what should be resisted?

Chapter Two: The Cycle

Reference: Judges 2:6–3:6

The Story We Tell Children

The Israelites kept forgetting God, so God let their enemies defeat them. When they cried out, God sent a judge to rescue them. Then they forgot again.

That's the version. It presents the cycle as a kind of spiritual forgetfulness that God patiently corrects. The text is asking harder questions than that.

The Slower Reading

1. The Cycle Is Not Random — It Is a Pattern of Choice

The narrator introduces the Deuteronomistic cycle at Judges 2:11–19 with unusual structural explicitness. This is not presented as a sequence of accidents. It is presented as a pattern: Israel abandons God, God withdraws protection, enemies oppress, Israel cries out, God raises a judge, judge delivers, rest, judge dies, Israel abandons God again — immediately, more thoroughly than before. The cycle is a formal structure. The narrator is giving the reader the interpretive key before the evidence is presented.

Judges 2:19 — And it came to pass, when the judge died, that they returned and corrupted themselves more than their fathers, in following other gods to serve them and to bow down to them. They ceased not from their own doings, nor from their stubborn way.

'More corrupt than their fathers' — the cycle does not level off. It descends. Each iteration goes further than the last. The book's structure reflects this: the judges grow more compromised, the deliverances more ambiguous, the moral landscape more degraded.

2. The Question the Cycle Raises About God

The cycle structure raises a theological question the book does not resolve: is God's mercy enabling the cycle? Israel sins, suffers, cries out, is rescued — and then sins again, now with the precedent that crying out works. Does grace become predictable? Does forgiveness become a license? The New Testament addresses this directly — Paul in Romans 6:1 asks 'Shall we continue in sin that grace may abound?' and answers

'By no means!' But Judges does not offer the rebuttal. It offers the evidence. Seventeen more chapters of it.

Judges 2:20–21 — And the anger of the LORD was kindled against Israel; and he said, Because this people has transgressed my covenant which I commanded their fathers, and has not obeyed my voice, I will no longer drive out any of the nations which Joshua left when he died.

3. A New Generation That Does Not Know

The cycle is initiated by a generational failure: 'there arose another generation after them who did not know the LORD or the work that he had done for Israel' (2:10). The Hebrew for 'know' here is *yada* — not merely intellectual acquaintance but covenantal relationship, the kind of knowing that involves loyalty and response. The generation that replaced the elders of Joshua's time did not simply forget facts. They lost the relational and covenantal framework within which the facts were intelligible.

Deuteronomy 6:4–9 commanded Israel to transmit this framework actively — to speak it to their children, to write it on their doorposts, to build it into the rhythm of daily life. The failure documented in Judges 2:10 is precisely the failure to do what Deuteronomy 6 required. The theological collapse is downstream of a pedagogical failure.

Legal-Canonical Framework

- **Deuteronomy 6:4–9** — the Shema and the command to active generational transmission

- **Deuteronomy 28** — the covenant blessings and curses whose pattern the cycle enacts

- **Leviticus 26:14–45** — the escalating consequences of covenant abandonment, which the cycle compresses into a repeating structure

New Testament Resonance

Paul's argument in Romans 1:18–32 traces a parallel descent — not cyclical but progressive — in which suppressing the knowledge of God leads to increasing moral darkness. The Judges cycle and Paul's spiral address the same phenomenon from different angles: what happens when a community systematically declines to maintain the relational and ethical framework it was given.

Hebrews 3:12–13 draws the direct application: *Take heed, brothers, lest there be in any of you an evil heart of unbelief, in departing from the living God. But exhort one another daily, while it is called today; lest any of you be hardened through the deceitfulness of sin.*

Discussion Questions

1. The cycle does not bottom out — each iteration is described as worse than the last. Does this change how you read the individual judge narratives? If the descent is structural, what does it mean to 'learn from' the stories of individual judges?

2. The generational failure in Judges 2:10 is a failure of transmission — the next generation did not *know* the LORD. What is the difference between knowing *about* God and the covenantal *yada* the text requires? What does active transmission of that kind of knowing look like in practice?

3. The cycle structure raises the question of whether God's mercy enables the pattern. How do you hold together the reality of genuine forgiveness with the warning that grace can be presumed upon? What does repentance that actually breaks the cycle look like, as opposed to remorse that restarts it?

4. The nations left in the land are described in 2:22 and 3:4 as serving a dual function: both a test of Israel's obedience and a snare that leads them into apostasy. Can difficulty and temptation serve a genuinely pedagogical purpose — and does that framing risk becoming an excuse for tolerating what should be resisted?

Chapter Three: Othniel — The Standard

Reference: Judges 3:7–11

The Story We Tell Children

Israel sinned, got oppressed, and God sent Othniel to rescue them. The Spirit of God came on him and he won. Peace for forty years.

That's the version. It presents Othniel as a minor figure — a warm-up act before the more interesting judges arrive. The text is doing the opposite. Othniel is not the prelude. He is the standard.

The Slower Reading

1. Eight Verses, One Function

The Othniel narrative is the shortest major judge account in the book. Eight verses. No dialogue. No complications. No named battle. No moral ambiguity. The cycle introduced in chapter two runs its first complete iteration, and it runs cleanly: Israel does evil, God gives them to an oppressor, they cry out, God raises a judge, the Spirit comes, the judge defeats the enemy, the land rests, the judge dies.

The brevity is not an accident of incomplete records. The author knows how to write a long judge narrative — the Gideon account runs two full chapters; Samson gets four. The compression here is intentional. Othniel is given exactly as much space as a flawless judge requires, which turns out to be eight verses. The implication is already working before the reader has noticed it.

2. The Pedigree and What It Signals

Othniel is introduced with unusual genealogical specificity. He is the son of Kenaz and the nephew — and, the text notes, the son-in-law — of Caleb. This is not filler. Caleb is the conquest generation's most faithful figure, the one man besides Joshua who urges the people to trust God when the spies return from Canaan with reports of giants. Caleb holds the line when the entire community breaks. Othniel is from Caleb's household, from Judah — the tribe that will eventually produce the monarchy, the tribe that opened the book by answering the call to go up first.

The genealogy is the author establishing as clearly as possible that Othniel is connected to the best of what the previous generation produced. He is not an outsider pressed into service. He is the generation that inherited faithfulness from a faithful man, and he delivers it.

Judges 3:9 — And when the children of Israel cried to the LORD, the LORD raised up a deliverer to the children of Israel, who delivered them, even Othniel the son of Kenaz, Caleb's younger brother.

3. The Spirit, the Judgment, the War

Three things happen in rapid succession: the Spirit of the LORD is upon Othniel, he judges Israel, and he goes to war. The sequence matters. The Spirit precedes the military action — the empowerment is for the whole task, not only the battle. The judging comes before the warfare. Othniel is not simply a warrior who wins; he is an instrument of the covenant operating as it was designed to operate.

Every one of these elements will be distorted in the judges that follow. The Spirit will come upon Samson — a man pursuing a private vendetta under cover of a Nazirite vow he has already broken. The judging will become increasingly compromised by personal interest. The warfare will be waged for increasingly unclear reasons. By the time the book reaches Samson, 'deliverance' is accidental, a byproduct of one man's desire for revenge on the people who blinded him. The clarity of Judges 3:10 makes the distortion of Judges 16 visible.

Judges 3:10 — And the Spirit of the LORD came upon him, and he judged Israel, and went out to war: and the LORD delivered Cushan-rishathaim king of Mesopotamia into his hand.

4. The Land Rests

'The land had rest forty years.' This is the longest period of rest in the book. Othniel's deliverance produces more stability

than any judge who follows him. Ehud gets eighty years —
twice the rest — which may reflect the magnitude of that
deliverance, or may reflect a different kind of accounting. But
the rest periods shorten as the book progresses. Gideon's forty
years is followed by immediate apostasy when he is barely in
the ground. Samson's twenty-year judgeship produces no rest
period at all — the text simply notes that he judged Israel and
then records his death.

The trajectory is visible only because the baseline is
established here. Forty years. Land at rest. Judge dies. The
standard, set once, at the beginning, before the complications
begin.

Legal-Canonical Framework

- **Deuteronomy 6:10–12** — the warning against forgetting the LORD when the land is settled and comfortable, spoken directly into the rest periods Judges documents

- **Numbers 11:25–29** — the Spirit of the LORD distributed among the seventy elders; the pattern of Spirit-empowered leadership established in the wilderness and reactivated in the judges

- **Deuteronomy 17:14–20** — the law of the king, which anticipates and constrains the monarchy the book is moving toward; Othniel operates as judge without any of the royal distortions Deuteronomy warns against

- **Joshua 14:6–14** — Caleb's claim to Hebron, his faithfulness confirmed, the genealogical line from which Othniel descends established in the previous generation

New Testament Resonance

The New Testament does not engage Othniel directly, but Hebrews 11:32 places him in the same list as Gideon, Barak, Jephthah, and Samson — a list the author explicitly says is incomplete. The inclusion is not an endorsement of every action those figures took. It is an acknowledgment that faith operated through imperfect instruments across the whole history. Othniel is the one figure in that list who requires no qualification. He is the measure against which the others are implicitly assessed.

The pattern Othniel embodies — Spirit empowerment preceding rather than replacing obedience, deliverance oriented toward the community rather than the deliverer, faithful genealogy transmitted and enacted — maps onto Paul's description of spiritual gifts in 1 Corinthians 12. The gift is not the point. The body it serves is the point. Othniel fights for Israel. He does not fight for Othniel.

Discussion Questions

1. Othniel's account takes eight verses and presents no complications. What does it suggest about the book's priorities that the one uncomplicated judge gets the least space? What would a contemporary reader assume about narrative length and moral significance — and what does the Judges author's choice say about that assumption?

2. The Spirit of the LORD comes upon Othniel — and also, later, upon Samson, who violates his Nazirite vow and fights entirely for personal reasons. What does the Spirit's presence in both narratives tell us about how Judges understands divine empowerment? Does the Spirit's involvement imply endorsement of the deliverer's character?

3. Othniel is introduced through his relationship to Caleb — the conquest generation's most faithful figure. The last judge is Samson, a Danite who fights alone and dies pulling a pagan temple down on himself. What does the genealogical and tribal trajectory across the book suggest about how Judges understands communal memory and the transmission of faithfulness?

4. The land rests forty years after Othniel — the standard against which subsequent rest periods are measured. What does it mean to establish a baseline before documenting a descent? How does reading Othniel first change how you read Samson last?

Chapter Four: Ehud — The Left-Handed Assassin

Reference: Judges 3:12–30

The Story We Tell Children

Israel was oppressed by a fat Moabite king named Eglon for eighteen years. God raised up Ehud, who killed the king in a clever way and led Israel to victory.

That's the version. It presents Ehud as a clever hero and moves quickly past the scatological detail. The text is doing something significantly more complicated — and considerably funnier — than the children's version allows.

The Slower Reading

1. The Text Is Satirizing the Oppressor

The Ehud narrative is written with unmistakable irreverence. Eglon's name in Hebrew is related to the word for calf — a word with significant connotations in a culture where golden calves represent apostasy. He is described as "a very fat man." The assassination scene is described with physical grotesquery: the blade disappears into the fat, the handle follows, and the narrator notes that Eglon's fat closes over the hilt. When the servants wait outside, they assume the king is "relieving himself" — a Hebrew idiom that means exactly what it sounds like. The narrative lingers on all of this. The author is writing political satire.

This creates an immediate interpretive question: if the text is satirizing the oppressor, what is it doing with the deliverer?

2. Ehud Operates Through Deception

Ehud's method of access depends on deception at multiple levels. He gains a private audience under the pretext of a secret message from God. He presents tribute that lulls the court into security. He has hidden a weapon on the side guards would not check — because he is left-handed, the sword is on his right thigh, the unexpected side. The narrator presents all of this as effective without offering a moral assessment. The text neither condemns nor celebrates the deception — it simply records that it worked.

This is the first instance of a pattern that will recur across Judges: the deliverer uses morally compromised means. The question the text raises — and does not answer — is whether the ends justify the means, or whether the method reveals something about the deliverer that the deliverance obscures.

Judges 3:20–22 — *Ehud said, "I have a message from God for you." And he arose from his seat. And Ehud reached with his left hand, took the sword from his right thigh, and thrust it into his belly. And the hilt also went in after the blade, and the fat closed over the blade, for he did not pull the sword out of his belly.*

3. What the Text Endorses and What It Leaves Open

The Ehud narrative celebrates the deliverance. The Moabites are defeated. Israel has peace for eighty years — twice the rest period of Othniel, which may reflect the relative magnitude of the achievement, or may reflect ambiguity accumulating in the institution. What the text does not provide is a direct assessment of Ehud's methods. The assassination of a foreign oppressor using deception is presented as effective and as God's instrument — but the Torah's framework around deception (Leviticus 19:11, Proverbs 12:22) does not disappear because the target was an enemy king.

The chapter should resist the temptation to flatten this into either "Ehud was wrong to lie" or "Ehud was justified because the cause was just." The text holds the tension open. The reader is meant to feel both the satisfaction of the liberation and the unease of the method — because that tension will intensify in every subsequent judge.

Legal-Canonical Framework

- **Leviticus 19:11** — "You shall not steal, neither deal falsely, neither lie one to another."

- **Proverbs 12:22** — " Lying lips are an abomination to the LORD, but those who deal truly are his delight."

- **Genesis 27; 37:31–33** — the Torah's own record of deception operating within the covenant line. Jacob deceives Isaac. Joseph's brothers deceive Jacob. The pattern is established long before Ehud, and the text's refusal to adjudicate in those cases carries forward here. The tension is structural, not incidental.

- **Deuteronomy 20:1–4** — the laws of holy war, which address the conditions under which Israel is to engage enemies, but do not include a deception provision. The narrator does not invoke this framework. Its absence is notable.

New Testament Resonance

Jesus' statement "let your yes be yes and your no be no" (Matthew 5:37) and Paul's "putting away falsehood, let each one of you speak the truth with his neighbor" (Ephesians 4:25) form the New Testament end of the canonical frame. The question Ehud's narrative raises — does the moral framework around deception apply when the cause is just? — receives no exemption in either testament.

What the New Testament adds is the category of enemies: love them (Matthew 5:44), pray for them, do not repay evil for evil (Romans 12:17). Ehud's narrative predates this framework; the Christian reader must hold both in view. The New Testament does not retroactively endorse Ehud's method. It also does not ignore the liberation he accomplished. The two facts coexist in the canon without being harmonized — which is precisely the interpretive situation the reader of Judges must learn to inhabit.

Discussion Questions

1. The Ehud narrative is written as political satire — Eglon's name, his obesity, and the scatological detail of his death are clearly deliberate. What does this narrative register — satire, dark comedy — suggest about the range of tones the biblical text uses to address oppression and liberation? What do we lose when we flatten Scripture into a single, reverent register?

2. Ehud's method depends entirely on deception. The text presents this as effective without offering a direct moral assessment. Does the effectiveness of a method justify its use? How does your answer change depending on whether the context is personal conflict, political resistance, or warfare?

3. The servants assume Eglon is relieving himself and wait politely outside — their deference to their king's privacy allows the assassin to escape. What does this detail suggest about how power structures enable their own undoing? Where do you see similar dynamics — deference, assumption, closed doors — protecting the wrong things today?

4. Ehud rallies Israel after the assassination — "Follow me, for the LORD has given your enemies the Moabites into your hand." How much does the moral character of the leader affect the validity of the cause they champion? Can a compromised instrument serve a legitimate mission?

Chapter Five: Deborah and Barak — The Prophetess and the Reluctant General

Reference: Judges 4–5

The Story We Tell Children

God raised up a woman named Deborah to lead Israel. A general named Barak helped her. They defeated a Canaanite army and a woman named Jael killed the enemy general.

That's the version. It renders Deborah benign, Barak cooperative, and Jael's act as straightforward heroism. The text is making an argument about authority, honor, and the violation of sacred obligations that the children's version does not transmit.

The Slower Reading

1. Deborah Is Already Judging Before the Crisis

The text introduces Deborah not as someone raised up in response to the oppression but as someone already functioning as a judge in Israel: "She used to sit under the palm of Deborah between Ramah and Bethel in the hill country of Ephraim, and the people of Israel came up to her for judgment" (4:5). This is not a crisis appointment. It is an established role. Deborah has authority before Barak enters the narrative. The question of whether a woman can hold judicial and prophetic authority in Israel is answered before it is asked — the text simply describes what she was already doing.

The later debates about women in leadership roles — debates conducted with significant force in both Jewish and Christian interpretation — have to contend with the fact that the narrator of Judges presents Deborah's authority as given, not questioned, not exceptional, and not explained. She judges. She prophesies. She commands. The text moves on.

Judges 4:4–5 — And Deborah, a prophetess, the wife of Lapidoth, judged Israel at that time. And she dwelt under the palm tree of Deborah between Ramah and Bethel in mount Ephraim: and the children of Israel came up to her for judgment.

2. Barak's Reluctance and the Transfer of Honor

Deborah summons Barak with a direct command from the LORD: "Go, gather your men at Mount Tabor... and I will give Sisera into your hand." Barak's response is conditional: "If you will go with me, I will go, but if you will not go with me, I will not go." The response is not presented as cowardice — Barak goes on to command the battle effectively. He is named in

Hebrews 11's hall of faith. But his conditional obedience is presented as the precise reason the honor of the victory will not be his.

Deborah's reply is precise: "I will surely go with you. Nevertheless, the road on which you are going will not lead to your glory, for the LORD will sell Sisera into the hand of a woman." This prophecy is fulfilled by Jael, not Deborah — but the logic is the same. The general who conditions his obedience on the presence of the prophet forfeits the honor that unconditional obedience would have received. The text is making an argument about what it means to fully trust a divine command.

Notice the contrast with Othniel. The Spirit came upon him; he judged; he went to war. No conditions. No negotiation. The degradation of the pattern that began with Ehud's deception continues here with Barak's reluctance. The deliverer is becoming less certain, more hedged, more dependent on external reassurance. The arc of the book is visible in the small details.

Judges 4:8–9 — And Barak said to her, If you will go with me, then I will go: but if you will not go with me, then I will not go. And she said, I will surely go with you: notwithstanding, the journey that you take shall not be for your honor; for the LORD shall deliver Sisera into the hand of a woman.

3. Jael: Savior and Covenant Violator

Jael's act is the chapter's most complex theological problem. She kills Sisera — and is celebrated for it in the Song of Deborah (5:24: "Most blessed of women be Jael, the wife of Heber the Kenite, of tent-dwelling women most blessed"). But she does so by violating one of the most fundamental obligations in ancient Near Eastern culture: the law of hospitality. Sisera comes to her tent as a refugee. She invites him in, gives him milk, covers him — all acts of protection and welcome. Then she drives a tent peg through his temple while he sleeps.

The Song praises the act. The prose narrative simply records it. Neither offers a moral evaluation. The reader is left holding the tension: this act saved Israel, was prophesied as a victory for a woman, and is celebrated in one of the oldest pieces of Hebrew poetry in the canon — and it was accomplished through the deliberate violation of a sacred obligation.

The hospitality laws are not peripheral. Genesis 18–19 establishes the protection of guests as a foundational covenant expectation; the wickedness of Sodom is crystallized precisely in the violation of that obligation. Leviticus 19:33–34 extends the protection explicitly to strangers. Sisera was under Jael's protection. The Song celebrates what the Torah prohibits.

The chapter should resist the temptation to resolve this tension. The celebration is in the canon. So is the prohibition. The reader must hold both.

Judges 5:24, 26–27 — Blessed above women shall Jael the wife of Heber the Kenite be, blessed shall she be above women in the tent... She put her hand to the nail, and her right hand to the workmen's hammer; and with the hammer she smote Sisera, she smote off his head, when she had pierced and stricken through his temples.

4. Two Versions of the Same Story

Judges 4 (prose) and Judges 5 (the Song of Deborah) tell the same story with meaningful differences, and the final form of the book includes both. In the prose, Barak pursues Sisera's fleeing army and Sisera escapes on foot to Jael's tent. In the

Song, the stars fight from their courses and the river Kishon sweeps the enemy away — cosmic participation in the battle that the prose does not mention.

The Song of Deborah is almost certainly older than the prose account. Its archaic Hebrew grammatical forms — the verbal patterns, the pronoun usage, the poetic syntax — are among the oldest attested in the biblical corpus, comparable in antiquity to the Song of the Sea in Exodus 15. The prose may be a later narrative expansion of events the Song originally preserved. The editor of the final Judges text chose to include both, placing the older poem after the prose account and inviting the reader to notice where they diverge.

One divergence is worth examining in detail: the role of the Kishon river. In the prose, the defeat of Sisera's nine hundred iron chariots is attributed to the LORD "routing Sisera and all his chariots and all his army before Barak." The Song attributes it differently:

Judges 5:20–21 — They fought from heaven; the stars in their courses fought against Sisera. The river of Kishon swept them away, that ancient river, the river Kishon.

The Song's version is not simply poetic decoration. It describes a cosmological event — the stars as divine agents, the river as an instrument of judgment — that the prose does not record. The most likely historical reconstruction is that a flash flood rendered the Canaanite chariots immobile in the valley of Jezreel, turning their iron advantage into a liability. The prose elides the mechanism. The Song preserves the cosmic interpretation: this was not just military action. The created order fought on Israel's side.

What the two versions together establish is that the text is not a single, uniform account. It is a conversation between traditions. The reader who has only the prose is missing what the Song preserves. The reader who has only the Song is missing the narrative logic the prose supplies. The canon gives both — and asks the reader to hold them together.

5. Sisera's Mother

The Song closes with an image that has no parallel in the prose account and that is one of the most theologically significant moments in the chapter: Sisera's mother waiting at her window.

Judges 5:28–30 — The mother of Sisera looked out at a window, and cried through the lattice, Why is his chariot so long in coming? why tarry the wheels of his chariots? Her wise ladies answered her, yes, she returned answer to herself, Have they not found, have they not divided the spoil; a damsel or two to every man; to Sisera a prey of divers colors, a prey of divers colors of needlework, of divers colors of needlework on both sides, fit for the necks of those who take the spoil?

The Song's poet imagines this woman. The enemy's mother. She does not know her son is dead. She is waiting for a victory that will not come, consoling herself with the anticipation of plunder — which the poem presents unflinchingly, including the "womb or two" that represents enslaved women taken as spoil. This is what the Canaanite victory would have meant. This is the world Jael's act prevented.

And yet the poet allows her grief. She is imagined with enough specificity — the lattice, the waiting, the self-consoling rationale — that her anguish is real. The Song celebrates the victory and mourns the cost simultaneously, across enemy lines. This is not sentimentality. It is the poem insisting that the human stakes of war are borne by people on both sides, including the people who deserve to lose.

Legal-Canonical Framework

- **Leviticus 19:33–34** — "And if a stranger sojourns with you in your land, you shall not vex him... you shall love him as yourself." The law that Jael violates. The celebration of her act in the Song does not dissolve the legal framework — it sits alongside it in permanent tension.

- **Genesis 18–19** — The hospitality narratives that establish guest protection as a covenant obligation. Abraham's welcome of the three strangers and Lot's defense of his guests form the narrative precedent. Sisera is the inversion of those guests; Jael is the inversion of those hosts. The echo is structural.

- **Numbers 12:1–8** — Moses' sister Miriam holds a prophetic role and leads in song after the Exodus; Deborah operates in the same tradition. The text in both cases neither explains nor apologizes for the female prophetic voice. It records it.

- **Proverbs 31** — The *eshet chayil*, the woman of valor, runs through Hebrew wisdom literature as an established category. Deborah and Jael are its narrative exemplars in Judges: one who judges and commands, one who delivers through unconventional strength.

- **Exodus 15** — The Song of the Sea, which the Song of Deborah echoes in structure, register, and function. Both are victory songs celebrating divine intervention in battle, both preserved in archaic Hebrew, both featuring women's voices (Miriam in Exodus, Deborah as author in Judges). The canonical pair invites the reader to see Deborah's song as standing in the great tradition of Israel's liturgical memory.

41

New Testament Resonance

Hebrews 11:32 places Barak in the faith hall of fame —
alongside Gideon, Jephthah, and Samson. The inclusion is
carefully calibrated: it acknowledges his faith in going to
battle, without endorsing the condition he attached to his
obedience. Hebrews 11's list is explicit that it describes people
whose faith was real and whose records were mixed. Barak
belongs in both categories.

The debate about women's authority in the church —
conducted across centuries with considerable force in both
directions — has frequently been carried on without full
engagement with the canonical picture Judges 4–5
contributes. Philip's daughters prophesy (Acts 21:9). Paul
acknowledges women prophesying in the gathered assembly
(1 Corinthians 11:5). Priscilla teaches (Acts 18:26). The New
Testament's picture is not uniform, and the debates are
genuine. But Deborah is a data point that cannot be removed
from the canonical record without distortion. She judged. The
text presents this as established fact, not exceptional
circumstance, not explained or defended. Any argument that
the biblical tradition categorically excludes women from
judicial or authoritative roles has to reckon with Judges 4:4–
5.

Jael's act raises the question Paul addresses in Romans 3:8 —
"why not do evil that good may come?" — from the other
direction. Paul is addressing the argument that sinning to
enable grace is justified. Jael is not sinning to enable grace;
she is violating a hospitality law to enable national
deliverance. The canon's silence on the moral verdict is
consistent: it does not adjudicate. It presents both the
celebration and the framework and leaves the reader in the
tension.

Discussion Questions

1. Deborah is presented as already judging Israel before the crisis that requires a military response. The text introduces her authority as established fact, not exceptional circumstance. What does this do to arguments that the biblical tradition categorically excludes women from judicial or authoritative roles? What interpretive work would be required to read Deborah as an exception rather than a precedent?

2. Barak's reluctance is not condemned outright — he fights, he wins, he is named in Hebrews 11. But his conditional obedience costs him the honor of the victory. Where in your own life or community do you see conditional obedience — saying "yes, but only if..." to things that don't require the condition? What is the cost of the condition?

3. Jael is celebrated in the Song for an act that violated the law of hospitality. The text holds both the celebration and the violation simultaneously without resolving the tension. What does it mean for Scripture to celebrate something morally complicated? How should we read texts that seem to endorse an act that other texts prohibit?

4. The Song of Deborah closes with Sisera's mother waiting at her window, imagining her son returning with plunder and enslaved women. The poet imagines the enemy's grief with specificity and empathy — while also naming exactly what Sisera's victory would have meant for Israel's women. What does it mean to mourn the cost of a necessary defeat? What does this image ask of the reader?

5. The prose account and the Song of Deborah tell the same story with meaningful differences. The final form of the canon includes both without harmonizing them. What does it mean for inspired Scripture to preserve two versions of an event that do not fully agree? What does this suggest about how the canon expects to be read?

Chapter Six: Gideon — The Pivot

Reference: Judges 6–8

The Story We Tell Children

Gideon was a humble farmer whom God chose to rescue Israel from Midian. He asked for a sign to confirm God's call — the famous fleece. God reduced his army from 32,000 to 300 to show that the victory belonged to God. They defeated Midian with torches and trumpets. Gideon refused to be king because God is Israel's king.

That's the version. It ends at Gideon's famous refusal of kingship — and stops there. The chapter doesn't end there. What follows the famous refusal is the thing the children's version cannot hold.

The Slower Reading

1. The Fear That Precedes the Faith

The angel of the LORD finds Gideon not standing in the open, not leading his people, but threshing wheat in a winepress — hiding it from the Midianites (6:11). The first image of Gideon is a man performing agricultural labor in secret, in a place designed for the wrong function, out of fear. The angel's greeting — *"The LORD is with you, O mighty man of valor"* — is ironic before it is prophetic. Gideon is not yet what the angel calls him. The name is a declaration of what he will become, not a description of what he is.

Gideon's first response is not gratitude but complaint: *"Please, my lord, if the LORD is with us, why then has all this happened to us?"* He questions the theological premise of the greeting. He catalogues the national suffering. He is presented not as a man of confident faith but as a man with legitimate grievances about the gap between what God is supposed to be doing and what is actually happening.

This matters for how the whole narrative is read. Gideon does not begin in doubt and arrive at faith. He moves through cycles of both, simultaneously, throughout all three chapters. The doubt and the faith coexist. They never fully resolve. The man who commands three hundred soldiers with torches and clay jars is the same man who will need a second fleece reading before he can take the field.

Judges 6:12–13 — And the angel of the LORD appeared to him, and said to him, The LORD is with you, you mighty man of valor. And Gideon said to him, O my Lord, if the LORD is with us, why then is all this befallen us?

2. The Signs and What They Reveal

Gideon demands multiple confirming signs — the fleece wet then dry; dry then wet; the angel who disappears in the altar flame; the direct night vision at Peor. The popular reading presents these as exemplary faith — bold enough to ask God for confirmation. The text presents them as something more complicated. Each sign is given. Each sign is followed by another request.

The fleece sequence is particularly instructive. Gideon does not ask once and trust. He asks, receives, then asks again — this time with the conditions inverted to rule out coincidence. *"Let it be dry on the fleece only, and on all the ground let there be dew"* (6:39). He apologizes for asking again even as he asks again. The apology does not prevent the second request. The pattern is not boldness. It is a man who needs the reassurance renewed because it does not hold.

This is not a condemnation. The Psalms document doubt extensively and without apology. Elijah collapses under a broom tree and asks to die. Moses argues with God at the burning bush. The biblical tradition is not sanitized of human reluctance. But the signs Gideon demands are signs he will not fully act on — he still needs the dream in the Midianite camp (7:10–15) before he can commit. The signs produce temporary confidence, not lasting transformation. The crucial question is not whether Gideon doubted — it is what the doubt costs. The narrator will show us the answer in chapters 7 and 8.

Judges 6:36–37 — And Gideon said to God, If you will save Israel by my hand, as you have said, behold, I will put a fleece of wool on the floor; and if the dew be on the fleece only...

3. The Reduction of the Army

The narrative's most famous episode — the reduction from 32,000 to 10,000 to 300 — is frequently read as an encouraging lesson about God's sufficiency over human weakness. The lesson is present. But the mechanics of the reduction deserve attention.

The first reduction is straightforward: the fearful may go home (7:3). Twenty-two thousand leave. Ten thousand remain. The second reduction is stranger. God instructs Gideon to bring the men to the water and separate those who lap like a dog from those who kneel to drink. Three hundred lap. Nine thousand seven hundred kneel. The lappers stay.

No explanation is given for the selection criterion. The text does not say the lappers were more alert, more warrior-like, or more faithful. It says God chose by this method specifically *"so that Israel may not boast over me, saying, 'My own hand has saved me'"* (7:2). The selection criterion is arbitrary by design. The victory is not supposed to follow from the quality of the soldiers. It is supposed to follow from the presence of God. The men who remain are too few to take credit.

This divine logic — deliberately underpowering the deliverer — is one of the sharpest theological moves in the book. It will echo in Paul's theology of weakness in 2 Corinthians. It stands in permanent tension with the human instinct to field the best available force. What the Midian campaign establishes is that "best available" is precisely not the point.

Judges 7:2 — *The LORD said to Gideon, "The people with you are too many for me to give the Midianites into their hand, lest Israel boast over me, saying, 'My own hand has saved me.'"*

4. The Refusal of Kingship — and What Immediately Follows

After the victory, the people offer Gideon dynastic rule: *"Rule over us, you and your son and your grandson also, for you have saved us from the hand of Midian"* (8:22). Gideon's refusal is theologically impeccable: *"I will not rule over you, and my son will not rule over you; the LORD will rule over you"* (8:23). It is one of the clearest anti-monarchic statements in the entire Hebrew Bible. It is the verse most often quoted when Gideon is held up as a model of humble, God-centered leadership.

The next verse — the very next verse — Gideon asks for a share of the plunder's gold earrings. The request is framed as modest: just the earrings, nothing from the camels or the personal ornaments of the kings. The people comply eagerly. The tally comes to 1,700 shekels of gold, plus the ornaments, pendants, and purple garments of the Midianite kings.

Gideon makes an ephod from this gold and places it in his hometown, Ophrah.

Judges 8:27 — And Gideon made it into an ephod, and put it in his city, even in Ophrah: and all Israel went there astray after it: which thing became a snare to Gideon and to his house.

The ephod is the priestly garment of inquiry — the mechanism by which God's will was discerned. It is not generically idolatrous in the way a carved image is idolatrous. It is a divination instrument, a means of access to divine guidance, associated with the legitimate priesthood. What Gideon has done is build a private version and install it in his hometown. He has not established a foreign god. He has established a private shrine to the God of Israel — centered on himself, located in Ophrah, drawing all of Israel to come to him.

The narrator's verdict is unsparing. This is whoring. It is a snare. And it snares not only Israel but Gideon's own family. The man who said *"the LORD will rule"* has built something that positions Gideon as the mediating center.

The gap between verse 23 and verse 27 is the gap the whole chapter has been building toward. It is not that Gideon's refusal was insincere. It is that the refusal operated at the level of title and office while the underlying hunger for centrality — for being the person people come to, for being the hinge on which Israel's access to God turns — was left unexamined. He declined the crown. He accepted everything the crown represents.

5. The Cruelty the Children's Version Omits

The victory over Midian is not clean. After the rout, Gideon pursues the Midianite kings Zebah and Zalmunna across the Jordan. He passes through Succoth and Penuel, towns of Israelite territory, and asks them for provisions for his exhausted troops. Both towns refuse — hedging their bets on whether Gideon will actually succeed. Gideon responds with a specific promise: *"When the LORD has given Zebah and Zalmunna into my hand, I will flail your flesh with the thorns of the wilderness and with briers"* (8:7).

He keeps the promise. After capturing the kings, he returns to Succoth, punishes the seventy-seven elders with thorns and briers, and tears down the tower of Penuel, killing the men of the city.

The punishment of towns that refused to support a campaign in progress — particularly towns in Israel's own territory — is not presented as divinely commanded. It is presented as

Gideon's personal retribution. The victory God gave him has become the instrument of a personal vendetta. The judge has begun exercising royal prerogatives: punishment of domestic enemies, accumulation of war spoils, establishment of a cult site. He has refused the title while assuming the function.

There is also the matter of the Midianite kings themselves. Gideon's pursuit of Zebah and Zalmunna is motivated partly by a specific personal grievance: they killed his brothers at Tabor (8:18–19). The battle that began as national deliverance ends as a blood feud. Gideon kills the kings himself, which is also a royal act — the disposition of captured enemies belongs to kings, not judges.

---

6. The Legacy: Abimelech

Gideon has seventy sons from many wives. The many wives are a detail that should not pass unnoticed — Deuteronomy 17:17 explicitly prohibits the king from multiplying wives, and the seventy sons who result are a dynastic structure in everything but name. He also has one additional son — Abimelech, son of a Shechemite concubine — by a woman who is not one of his wives.

Gideon dies. Abimelech, leveraging his Canaanite maternal lineage, secures funding from the temple of Baal-Berith — seventy silver pieces, one for each brother — hires worthless men, and murders sixty-nine of his brothers on a single stone. He becomes the closest thing to a king Israel has yet produced.

The man who refused a crown has fathered the man who seizes it.

This is Judges' argument about legacy: what you decline in your own life may be precisely what you pass to the next generation — especially if the declining was verbal rather than structural. Gideon said the right words. His household told a different story. The children's version ends with the famous refusal. The text ends with the blood on the stone.

Judges 9:5 — And he went to his father's house at Ophrah, and slew his brothers the sons of Jerubbaal, being seventy persons, on one stone: notwithstanding yet Jotham the youngest son of Jerubbaal was left; for he hid himself.

Legal-Canonical Framework

- **Deuteronomy 17:14–20** — The law of the king, which prohibits the accumulation of horses, wives, and gold. Gideon's camels, multiple wives, and 1,700 shekels of gold check each of these boxes precisely. He has become the thing the law warns against without accepting the title that would have made the prohibition explicit.

- **Exodus 20:4–5; Leviticus 19:4** — Prohibitions against carved images and objects of idolatrous veneration. The ephod functions as a substitute shrine — a mechanism for divine inquiry that has been separated from the legitimate priestly structure and installed in a private location for private benefit.

- **Deuteronomy 13:1–5** — Warnings about leaders who use signs and wonders to draw Israel away from the covenant. Gideon does not draw Israel to a foreign god. He draws them to an unauthorized form of access to Israel's God — which the text treats with equal severity.

- **Numbers 27:21** — The legitimate use of the ephod for divine inquiry was mediated through the priest Eleazar using the Urim and Thummim. Gideon's ephod bypasses the entire priestly apparatus and locates divine consultation in Ophrah, with himself as the apparent mediating figure.

- **Deuteronomy 12:5–7** — The command to worship only at the place the LORD chooses, not at private locations established by individuals. Ophrah is not that place. The ephod shrine is a structural violation of centralized worship regardless of its intentions.

New Testament Resonance

James 1:6–8 addresses the double-minded man who asks in faith but wavers — *"he is like a wave of the sea, driven and tossed by the wind... unstable in all his ways."* Gideon is the Old Testament portrait of the double-minded deliverer: genuine faith coexisting with persistent doubt, real victory followed immediately by idolatrous legacy. The double-mindedness does not disqualify him from being used. It does not prevent the victory. What it produces is instability in the structures he leaves behind.

Paul's statement in 2 Corinthians 12:9 — *"my grace is sufficient for you, for my power is made perfect in weakness"* — is the theological frame that Gideon's narrative inhabits without resolving. God used Gideon's weakness. The 300 defeated the Midianites. The land had rest for forty years. None of that is diminished. But the weakness was not merely the instrument of God's glory — it was also the seedbed of the snare. Paul's theology does not promise that weakness used by God has no downstream consequences. Gideon's story is evidence for what those consequences can look like.

Hebrews 11:32 names Gideon in the faith hall of fame, alongside figures whose records are explicitly described as mixed. The inclusion is not an endorsement of the ephod or the retribution at Succoth or the seventy sons or the concubine in Shechem. It is an acknowledgment that faith and failure are not mutually exclusive categories, and that the same life can contain both in proportions that resist easy summary.

The gap between Gideon's stated theology and his structural behavior — *"the LORD will rule"* followed by the construction of a private cult center — anticipates Jesus' diagnosis in Matthew 15:8: *"This people draws near to me with their mouth, and honors me with their lips; but their heart is far from me."* The problem is not that Gideon did not believe what he said. The problem is that what he said and what he built were operating on different premises. The lips and the hands told different stories.

Discussion Questions

1. Gideon's first image is a man threshing wheat in a winepress, hiding from the enemy. The angel calls him *"a mighty man of valor."* What does it mean to be addressed by what you are becoming rather than what you currently are? When has someone named something in you that felt more like a promise than a description — and what did that naming cost them to say and you to receive?

2. The army is reduced from 32,000 to 300 specifically so that Israel cannot boast of its own strength. The selection criterion — how the men drink water — is not a test of quality or faithfulness; it is deliberately arbitrary. What does this divine logic say about how God relates to human achievement? Where does this principle create problems for how we typically evaluate success, strategy, or competence in communities of faith?

3. Gideon demands multiple signs, receives them, and then needs another. The signs produce temporary confidence, not lasting transformation. What is the difference between asking God for confirmation and asking God for what you need to act *without* further confirmation? Where does the line between faithful discernment and the refusal to commit actually fall?

4. Gideon refuses kingship in one verse and builds a private cult object in the next. How do you account for the gap between a person's stated theology — *"the LORD will rule"* — and the structures they actually build? Where do you see this gap, between what leaders

say and what institutions they create, operating in communities today?

5. The ephod becomes a snare for *"all Israel"* and for Gideon's family. Gideon's most famous moment — the refusal of kingship — did not prevent his most damaging act — the creation of a private shrine. What does this suggest about the relationship between individual moments of faithfulness and the systemic patterns that outlast them?

6. Gideon's son Abimelech murders sixty-nine brothers and seizes the kingship his father refused. How does the Gideon-Abimelech sequence change your reading of Gideon's refusal? Does the famous moment of humility look different once you see what it failed to prevent? What does this suggest about the relationship between a leader's public words and their private household?

Chapter Seven: Abimelech — The Anti-Judge

Reference: Judges 9

The Story We Tell Children

Gideon's son Abimelech wanted to be king. He killed his brothers and ruled Shechem for a while, but then God caused trouble between him and the people, and he was eventually killed when a woman dropped a millstone on him.

That's the version. It presents Abimelech as a villain who got his comeuppance. The chapter contains the first extended political fable in the Bible and the sharpest anti-monarchic argument in all of Judges — neither of which the children's version transmits.

The Slower Reading

1. The Name — and the Irony

Abimelech means *my father is king*. The man whose name announces royal lineage is the son of a man who famously refused to be king. The irony is structural: Gideon's verbal denial of kingship was immediately followed by behavior indistinguishable from proto-royal accumulation — multiple wives, seventy sons, a private cult center, personal vendettas executed with military force. His son's name announces the conclusion Gideon's life was already building toward. The anti-monarchic refusal produced the monarchic heir.

This is Judges' argument about legacy working at its most precise: what you decline in title, you may still transmit in structure. Gideon said the right words. His household told a different story. Abimelech is that different story made flesh.

2. The Fratricide on the Stone

Abimelech goes to his mother's relatives in Shechem and makes his pitch on the basis of kinship: *I am your bone and your flesh* (9:2). He leverages the Canaanite half of his identity — the half Gideon's household would have considered disqualifying — as a political asset. Shechem funds him from the temple of Baal-Berith: seventy pieces of silver, one for each brother.

He uses the money to hire *worthless and reckless men* — the Hebrew is *ṭōbh we-rēqîm*, empty men, the same descriptor used for the hired killers Abimelech recruited and the same social category Jephthah will later inhabit. With these men, he goes to Ophrah and murders sixty-nine of his brothers on a single stone. The one who escapes is Jotham, the youngest — who has no power and therefore no value as a threat.

The arithmetic of the exchange should not pass unnoticed. Seventy pieces of silver purchase the deaths of seventy men. The betrayal of blood is placed in a financial transaction, funded by a pagan temple treasury. The text draws no explicit moral. It does not need to. The numbers speak.

And he went to his father's house at Ophrah and killed his brothers the sons of Jerubbaal, seventy men, on one stone. But Jotham the youngest son of Jerubbaal was left, for he hid himself. — Judges 9:5

3. Jotham's Fable — Israel's First Political Satire

Jotham, the sole survivor, climbs to the top of Mount Gerizim — the mountain of blessing — and delivers the first extended political fable in the Hebrew Bible. The trees seek a king. They approach the olive tree first. The olive declines: *shall I leave my abundance, by which gods and men are honored, and go hold sway over the trees?* The fig tree is next. It declines: *shall I leave my sweetness and my good fruit and go hold sway over the trees?* Then the vine: *shall I leave my wine that cheers God and men and go hold sway over the trees?* Finally, the thornbush. The thornbush accepts — and immediately issues a threat: *If in good faith you are anointing me king over you, come and take refuge in my shade; but if not, let fire come out of the thornbush and devour the cedars of Lebanon.*

The fable's political logic is precise and devastating. The organisms with something to offer have better uses for their energy than rule. Power accrues to those who have nothing else to give. The thornbush is not a ruler by vocation; it is a vacuum-filler. And the thornbush does not simply accept — it immediately establishes conditional terms and threatens fire. The offer of shade from a thornbush is not nothing; it is ridiculous. Thornbushes do not provide meaningful shade. The offer is a performance of power by something incapable of its substance.

And the bramble said to the trees, 'If in good faith you are anointing me king over you, then come and take refuge in my shade, but if not, let fire come out of the bramble and devour the cedars of Lebanon.' — Judges 9:15

Jotham applies the fable directly: if Shechem and Abimelech have acted in good faith toward Gideon's house, then rejoice in your thornbush king. If not — let fire come out. Then he runs, because he has no army and no protection.

The rest of the chapter records the fire.

This is the first appearance of the problem that will consume the Samuel narratives and shadow the entire monarchy: what kind of king does a human community actually produce when left to its own political logic? The fable is not abstract. It is a diagnosis of what just happened and a forecast of what is coming.

4. Divine Retribution Through Political Discord

Three years into Abimelech's rule, *God sent an evil spirit between Abimelech and the leaders of Shechem* (9:23).

This is one of the more theologically uncomfortable verses in Judges, and the text offers no apology for it. God sends a spirit of discord — an evil spirit — to accomplish the dismantling of Abimelech's illegitimate power. The narrator frames this explicitly as divine justice: the evil spirit comes *so that the violence done to the seventy sons of Jerubbaal might come, and their blood be laid on Abimelech their brother, who killed them, and on the men of Shechem, who strengthened his hands to kill his brothers* (9:24).

The pattern established in the Deuteronomistic cycle — God uses outside nations to discipline Israel — extends here. God uses political dysfunction, internal betrayal, and civic collapse to dismantle a murderous ruler. The instrument is ugly. The text is not interested in sanitizing it. When legitimate structures fail and the thornbush is in power, the means available for justice are not clean.

Gaal son of Ebed arrives in Shechem and incites rebellion. Abimelech is tipped off, attacks at dawn, routs Gaal's forces, and retakes the city. He then destroys Shechem entirely and sows it with salt — a ritual declaration of permanent desolation. The citizens of the Tower of Shechem take refuge in the stronghold of the temple of El-Berith. Abimelech cuts wood, stacks it against the stronghold, and burns it. A thousand people die.

The thornbush promised fire. The thornbush delivered fire. On the people who installed it.

5. The Death — and What It Suppresses

Abimelech moves on to Thebez and besieges the city. The people flee into a strong tower. He approaches the tower door to set it on fire — the same method that worked at Shechem.

A woman on the tower drops an upper millstone on his head and fractures his skull.

His immediate response is not to deal with the wound. It is to manage the story. He commands his armor-bearer: *"Draw your sword and thrust me through, lest they say about me, 'A woman killed him.'"* His armor-bearer runs him through. Abimelech dies.

He spends his last breath trying to control the narrative of his death. He fails. The narrator records both the attempt at

suppression and the fact the attempt was made to conceal —
and then adds the theological verdict: *Thus God returned the
evil of Abimelech, which he committed against his father in
killing his seventy brothers. And God also made all the evil of
the men of Shechem return on their heads* (9:56–57).

The irony of his death at a woman's hand deliberately echoes
Sisera — the great Canaanite general killed by a woman,
whose death the Song of Deborah celebrated and refused to
spare Sisera the shame of. Abimelech did not want to be
Sisera. He took the same precautions Sisera took: he fled to
what he thought was safety, he believed he had survived, he
did not take the threat seriously. He became Sisera anyway.

The woman of Thebez is never named. Like Jael, like
Jephthah's daughter, like the concubine of Judges 19, she
enters the text to do what the men around her will not or
cannot do — and then the text moves on. The unnamed woman
ends the chapter the fable was predicting. The thornbush
caught fire.

The Numbered Wrongs

1. Abimelech manipulates ethnic identity as a political tool, exploiting his Canaanite lineage to secure resources from a pagan temple for violence against his own family.

2. He funds the murder of sixty-nine brothers with temple money — placing the betrayal of blood in a financial transaction.

3. He murders his brothers on a single stone, a ritual execution that echoes sacrifice — performed at Ophrah, the site of his father's unauthorized cult object.

4. He establishes himself as king by violence, without divine calling, without the Spirit of the LORD, without any of the mechanisms by which judges are raised up.

5. He destroys Shechem — an Israelite city — and sows it with salt, a permanent desolation reserved for the most hated enemies.

6. He burns the temple stronghold at Shechem with a thousand people inside.

7. He dies attempting to suppress the true account of his death, making narrative control his final act.

Legal-Canonical Framework

Deuteronomy 17:14–20 — The law of the king specifies what a king must not do: multiply horses, return to Egypt, multiply wives, or accumulate silver and gold to excess. Gideon's life checked each of these boxes without the title. Abimelech assumes the function of king — war-making, domestic punishment, civic destruction — also without the title. The chapter is what Deuteronomy 17 is warning against at the institutional level: kingship exercised without any of the covenantal constraints the law placed on it.

Deuteronomy 13:12–16 — The law concerning a city that has been drawn into apostasy and rebellion provides for its complete destruction: *you shall surely put the inhabitants of that city to the sword, devoting it to destruction, all who are in it and its livestock, with the edge of the sword.* Abimelech destroys Shechem — but for personal political revenge, not covenant faithfulness. He is performing the form of the law's most severe sanction for entirely self-interested reasons. The externals resemble obedience. The interior is pure vendetta.

Numbers 30:1–2; Ecclesiastes 5:4–6 — These passages govern vows and their weight. Gideon's legacy is built on an unauthorized cult object. Abimelech's inheritance is built on a vow of protection Gideon implicitly made to all seventy sons and never kept. The covenantal language of kinship — *I am your bone and your flesh* — is used by Abimelech to extract loyalty from Shechem, not to extend it to his brothers. The vocabulary of covenant is weaponized.

Genesis 4:10 — The voice of your brother's blood cries to me from the ground.

The seventy brothers on the stone are the most extensive fratricide in the Hebrew Bible to this point. The Cain pattern

— brother killing brother for position and recognition — is not an isolated act of origins. It is a structural tendency the text is tracking from Genesis through Judges. The number increases. The blood cries louder.

New Testament Resonance

Luke 14:28–33 — Jesus' parable of the man who builds a tower and fails to count the cost, and the king who goes to make war without first sitting down and consulting whether he is able to meet his enemy.

The parable's point is the necessity of honest reckoning before committing to a course of action. Abimelech is the negative space the parable describes: a man who seizes power without counting what it will cost the people around him, and whose project collapses because its foundations were blood, not covenant.

Matthew 20:25–28 — You know that the princes of the Gentiles exercise dominion over them, and they that are great exercise authority over them. But it shall not be so among you: but whoever will be great among you, let him be your servant.

Abimelech is the exhaustive demonstration of what Jesus is contrasting with the kingdom. Every move he makes — the ethnic leverage, the hired killers, the fratricide, the political consolidation, the military campaigns, the narrative suppression — is the Gentile ruler's logic applied without restraint. The text does not present this as surprising. It presents it as predictable. When you install a thornbush, fire is what you get.

Revelation 6:15–17 — The great men and the mighty men hid themselves in the dens and in the rocks of the mountains, calling on the mountains and rocks to fall on them, for the great day of wrath has come, and who shall be able to stand?

Abimelech, who destroyed the tower stronghold at Shechem by fire, dies approaching a tower. The instrument of his victory becomes the site of his end. The chapter has the shape of retribution so exact it reads as theological argument: the structures you build to destroy others are the structures that destroy you.

Discussion Questions

1. Jotham's fable argues that the most capable and productive leaders are too busy being valuable to seek power, and that power therefore accumulates in those with nothing better to do. How does this political analysis hold up against what you observe in leadership — in churches, organizations, institutions, politics? What conditions produce olive trees? What conditions produce thornbushes?

2. Abimelech funds his coup with money from a pagan temple. The fratricide is literally paid for by religious funds redirected to political violence. Where do you see religious resources — money, credibility, community trust, moral authority — used today to fund power grabs that have nothing to do with the stated purpose of those resources?

3. The text says God sent *an evil spirit* to introduce discord between Abimelech and Shechem. The narrator presents this as justice, not as a problem. How do you hold together a theology of God as the source of peace and unity with passages like this, where God deliberately introduces conflict to accomplish a just outcome? Does the end justify the means here — and if so, what does that do to your theology?

4. Abimelech's last act is an attempt to suppress the narrative of his death — to prevent the record from showing that a woman killed him. He fails. The narrator records both his attempt and the fact it was meant to conceal. What does this suggest about the relationship between power and control of story? What

happens when those who hold power cannot control how they are remembered?

5. Gideon's verbal refusal of kingship is one of the clearest anti-monarchic statements in the Hebrew Bible. Abimelech's existence is the chapter that answers it. What does the Gideon-Abimelech sequence together suggest about the relationship between what leaders say publicly and what they build privately — and about which one a community should trust?

Chapter Eight: Jephthah — The Vow and the Daughter

Reference: Judges 10:6–12:7

The Story We Tell Children

Jephthah was a mighty warrior who made a rash promise to God before a battle. He said he would sacrifice the first thing that came out of his house if God gave him victory. His daughter came out first. It was a tragedy.

That's the version. It presents Jephthah as a tragic hero who made an unlucky mistake. The text makes a far more uncomfortable argument — about vows, about daughters, about what the narrator refuses to name.

The Slower Reading

1. The Man Who Was Expelled and Returned

Jephthah's origin story is social marginalization. He is the son of a prostitute, expelled by his half-brothers when their father dies so that he will not share the inheritance. He goes to live in the land of Tob with *worthless men* — the same descriptor used for Abimelech's hired killers in the previous chapter. The vocabulary is not accidental. Israel's cycle has descended far enough that its next deliverer is recruited from the same social category as the previous chapter's villain.

When Ammon threatens Israel, the elders of Gilead come to retrieve the man they expelled. Jephthah's first act is not gratitude. It is negotiation. He will return if they make him head after the battle. He is transacting with the community that discarded him, and he is not pretending otherwise.

The irony is precise: Israel is in the cycle again, crying out to God, and God's instrument is a man society threw away. The chapter that follows will demonstrate that Jephthah has internalized the logic of that society more completely than the elders who expelled him understand.

Judges 11:2–3 — And Gilead's wife bore him sons; and his wife's sons grew up, and they thrust out Jephthah, and said to him, You shall not inherit in our father's house; for you are the son of a strange woman. Then Jephthah fled from his brothers, and dwelt in the land of Tob: and there were gathered vain men to Jephthah, and went out with him.

2. The Diplomacy That Failed

Before the battle, Jephthah attempts diplomacy with the Ammonite king — and the attempt is sophisticated. He offers a historical argument: Israel did not take Ammonite land; the land in question was taken from the Amorite king Sihon in a battle Ammon could have contested at the time and did not. He draws on Numbers 20–21 and Deuteronomy 2. He argues law. He argues precedent. He argues time.

The Ammonite king ignores it.

This matters for reading what comes next. Jephthah is not a man without intelligence or capacity for reason. He is capable of careful, structured argument — and then makes the worst possible decision under pressure. The diplomat who could construct a legal brief across three chapters of Torah cannot manage his own tongue before a battle.

3. The Vow and Its Catastrophe

If you give the Ammonites into my hands, whatever comes out of the door of my house to meet me when I return in triumph will be the LORD's, and I will sacrifice it as a burnt offering.

The vow is not unusual in form. Vows made in crisis are common in the ancient world, in Scripture, and in the Torah. Numbers 30 contains an elaborate system for managing vow obligations precisely because people make rash vows in foxholes and moments of desperation. The unusual element is the open-ended object. Any competent reading of ancient Israelite domestic life would recognize that the first thing out of the door might be a person — household members, especially women and daughters, were expected to meet returning warriors with celebration. Jephthah's formulation is reckless because it is not bounded.

His daughter comes out first, dancing with tambourines. She is his only child.

The text records no moment of horror or reconsideration on Jephthah's part. What it records is the tearing of garments and the words: *you have brought me very low.*

Judges 11:35 — And it came to pass, when he saw her, that he tore his clothes, and said, Alas, my daughter! you have brought me very low, and you are one of those who trouble me: for I have opened my mouth to the LORD, and I cannot go back.

Author's note: "You have brought me very low." The daughter has done nothing except come out of the door. Jephthah's framing places the catastrophe on her — his grief is about what she has cost him. This is not incidental. It is the chapter's sharpest indictment. The man who was socially discarded now performs the same displacement onto his child. His suffering becomes the narrative center; her fate becomes the context for his suffering.

4. The Core Interpretive Question

Did Jephthah literally sacrifice his daughter, or dedicate her to perpetual virginity — effectively ending her lineage?

The text is deliberately ambiguous. *He did to her as he had vowed* could mean either. The Hebrew mourning tradition for the daughter of Jephthah (11:40) might suggest she is dead, or might be a memorial for what was lost in her perpetual dedication. Scholars have argued this for centuries. The secondary literature is extensive, and the chapter should represent the strongest versions of both positions without pretending the ambiguity can be resolved.

But observe something the debate often misses: the text's deliberate ambiguity is itself the point. Whether she was killed or dedicated, the outcome is the same in the terms the narrative cares about — she is erased. She goes into the hills to *weep for her virginity*. She has no sons. She has no lineage. She has no name.

The debate about whether she was killed or merely disappeared has sometimes had the effect of reducing the atrocity to a technicality. Both outcomes, for a woman in this culture, represent her complete elimination. The legal distinction between literal sacrifice and forced celibacy matters enormously in every other register. In this text, the narrator's silence is a signal that it matters less than we want it to.

5. The Daughter's Namelessness

She is never named.

Like the concubine in chapter 19, she moves through one of the most consequential narratives in the book without a name. The text gives names to the Ammonite king. To the cities Jephthah punishes. To the Ephraimite soldiers tested at the ford. The person at the narrative's moral center is nameless.

This is not an accident of incomplete records. It is a literary and theological signal. The text is forcing the reader to feel what the community did not feel — that this person mattered. The namelessness is an indictment built into the grammar of the narrative.

What the daughter does with her unnamed two months is worth dwelling on. She does not argue. She does not appeal. She asks for time to mourn what she is losing — not her life, but her virginity, her future, her descendants. She grieves forward, into the absence of what she will never have. She grieves more honestly than her father, who grieves only for himself. She is the more dignified figure in their exchange, and the text makes sure we see this.

Judges 11:36–37 — And she said to her father, My father, if you have opened your mouth to the LORD, do to me according to that which has proceeded out of your mouth; forasmuch as the LORD has taken vengeance for you of your enemies, even of the children of Ammon. And she said to her father, Let this thing be done for me: let me alone two months, that I may go up and down upon the mountains, and bewail my virginity, I and my companions.

6. The Shibboleth and Civil War

The chapter does not end with the vow. It closes with Jephthah's inter-tribal violence.

Ephraim picks a quarrel: why weren't we included in the battle? Jephthah explains, correctly, that he did call them and they did not come. The Ephraimites escalate — calling the Gileadites *fugitives of Ephraim* (12:4). Jephthah's Gileadites seize the Jordan fords, and the test becomes phonological. Those from Ephraim cannot pronounce the *sh* sound. They say *Sibboleth* instead of *Shibboleth*. Forty-two thousand Ephraimites are killed at the crossing, identified by their dialect.

The *shibboleth* has entered English as a general term for any marker used to identify and exclude outsiders. In its original context, it is the chapter's closing demonstration of tribalism's logical endpoint: the man who began by negotiating his own return to community ends by killing Israelites for the way they speak. The deliverer who was expelled for being the wrong kind of person now makes dialect a death sentence.

Jephthah judged Israel for six years and died. The text gives him no theological epitaph. The cycle continues.

The Numbered Wrongs

- Jephthah makes a vow with an open-ended object in a context where any competent reader of Israelite domestic life would recognize the risk. The recklessness is not ignorance; it is pressure mismanaging an intelligence the diplomacy section demonstrated he possessed.

- When his daughter emerges, Jephthah's first words place the weight of the catastrophe on her: *you have brought me very low*. She came out the door. He made the vow. The displacement is the chapter's indictment in miniature.

- He does not avail himself of the Torah's explicit mechanism for redeeming rash vows. Leviticus 27 built a redemption provision into the vow system precisely for this situation. The price was set. The path existed. He does not take it.

- The daughter is not named. The text denies her the basic dignity of a name in a narrative that names her father's enemies, cities, and subordinates.

- The chapter closes not with the tragedy of the vow but with Jephthah killing forty-two thousand Israelites for their dialect. The man who was expelled for being the wrong kind of person has built a test of belonging that kills people for how they sound.

Legal-Canonical Framework

Leviticus 27:1–8 — The law of commuting vows: a human being dedicated to the LORD could be redeemed with a specified payment. The redemption mechanism exists. Jephthah does not use it.

Numbers 30 — The Torah's elaborate framework for managing vow obligations, including provisions for rash vows. Jephthah is not without legal alternatives. His failure to use them is not ignorance of the law — the diplomatic speech of 11:12–27 demonstrates his command of Torah. It is something more like theological rigidity: a belief that the vow, once spoken, is more binding than the law that provided for its release.

Deuteronomy 12:31 — You shall not do so to the LORD your God: for every abomination to the LORD, which he hates, have they done to their gods; for even their sons and their daughters they have burned in the fire to their gods.

If the literal reading of the vow is correct, Jephthah commits precisely what this law names as the characteristic abomination of the nations.

Ecclesiastes 5:2–5 — Be not rash with your mouth... Better is it that you should not vow, than that you should vow and not pay. Suffer not your mouth to cause your flesh to sin.

The Preacher is describing Jephthah in advance.

New Testament Resonance

Hebrews 11:32 lists Jephthah in the faith hall of fame —
alongside Gideon, Barak, and Samson. This is one of the most
difficult passages to hold alongside the narrative of the vow.
Hebrews is not endorsing the vow or its outcome. It is
acknowledging that Jephthah trusted God for military
deliverance — and Hebrews 11's larger argument is precisely
that faith operated through imperfect, sometimes
catastrophically flawed instruments across the entire history
of Israel. The chapter includes Rahab, a prostitute. It includes
Samson. The hall of fame is not a gallery of the morally
exemplary. It is a gallery of the ones who — in one specific
moment or dimension — trusted God rather than what they
could see. The canon preserves both realities: the faith and the
catastrophe. Neither cancels the other.

James 4:13–17 and **Matthew 5:33–37** address rash vows
from different angles: don't presume on the future, and don't
bind yourself unnecessarily to words that may cost more than
you know. *Let your yes be yes.* The New Testament's vow
theology reaches back to Jephthah as the terminus of what the
refusal of that counsel produces.

Discussion Questions

1. Jephthah is a skilled diplomat who makes a catastrophically rash vow. How do you account for the gap between demonstrated intelligence in one domain — legal and historical reasoning — and catastrophic judgment in another? Where do you see this pattern in leadership: competence in one register, devastating blind spots in another?

2. The Torah provided mechanisms for redeeming rash vows. Jephthah had options he did not take. What does his failure to use the available legal provisions tell us about his theology — what did he believe about the nature of the vow, and about God's relationship to it? Is there a version of faithfulness that becomes its own trap?

3. Jephthah's first words to his daughter are *you have brought me very low*. She came out the door. He made the vow. What does the displacement of responsibility onto the daughter reveal about his character — and about how narratives of loss are often constructed to protect the one with power?

4. The daughter is not named. Neither is the concubine in Judges 19. Neither is Samson's Timnite wife, who is also killed. The book's most devastating female victims are systematically anonymous. What is the theological and ethical weight of namelessness in a narrative? What does it demand of the reader to supply the dignity the text withholds?

5. The shibboleth test kills forty-two thousand Israelites for their dialect. It is the chapter's closing image — not the victory over Ammon, not the vow and its aftermath,

but the massacre of Israelites by Israel's own deliverer. What does this escalation suggest about where Jephthah's trajectory ends? What does it say about the relationship between personal trauma, power, and the violence we direct at our own communities?

6. Hebrews 11 names Jephthah among those commended for faith. How do you hold that alongside what the chapter records? What does it do to the category of *faith* to find it applied to a man whose trust in God for military deliverance coexists with a catastrophic failure to trust God's own law for relief from the vow?

Chapter Nine: Samson — The Consecrated and the Compromised

Reference: Judges 13–14

The Story We Tell Children

Samson was a special baby — an angel told his parents he would be born to deliver Israel from the Philistines. He had to follow special rules: no haircuts, no wine, no touching dead things. He grew up incredibly strong. When he fell in love with a Philistine woman, he killed a lion on the way to meet her, and later found honey in the lion's carcass. He made a riddle about it at his wedding feast, and his wife gave away the answer to his Philistine guests.

That's the version. It presents Samson as a strongman with a secret code. The text presents something more unsettling from the very first verse: a man whose consecration is announced before his birth and violated before his wedding feast, and a narrator who tells us God was working through the violation.

The Slower Reading

1. The Annunciation and What It Promises

Samson's birth narrative is the most formally developed in the book of Judges. An angel of the LORD appears to Manoah's wife — who is barren — and announces a child. The angel specifies the terms of the boy's consecration: no wine or strong drink, no unclean food, no razor on his head. He will be a Nazirite *from the womb*. He will begin to deliver Israel from the Philistines.

Three elements of this annunciation deserve attention.

The first is the woman. The angel appears to her, not to Manoah. She receives the message directly. When she reports it to her husband and he asks God to send the messenger again, the angel returns — again to the woman, alone in the field. Manoah is not present for either visit. He arrives secondhand, asks the angel to repeat himself, and promptly asks the wrong questions: what is your name, and what is the rule for the boy? The angel has already told his wife the rule. Manoah is catching up to a conversation his wife has already had. She sees more clearly than he does in nearly every exchange that follows.

The second is the word *begin*. He will *begin* to deliver Israel from the Philistines. Not complete. Not establish. Begin. The annunciation is already bounded. Whatever Samson does, it will not be finished — and the text is honest about this from the first oracle.

The third is the structure of the vow. Nazirite consecration in Numbers 6 is a voluntary act, taken for a specified period. Samson's Nazirite vow is not voluntary — it is imposed before birth, by divine declaration, with no term limit. He does not choose this. He is chosen into it. And the irony that will govern every chapter that follows is already present here: the vow imposes separation from the unclean, and Samson will spend his life moving toward the unclean as if drawn by gravity.

"For behold, you shall conceive and bear a son. No razor shall come upon his head, for the child shall be a Nazirite to God from the womb, and he shall begin to save Israel from the hand of the Philistines." — Judges 13:5

---

2. Manoah's Wife — The Chapter's Most Reliable Theologian

Before the Samson narrative begins in earnest, the text gives us a scene that functions as quiet calibration: Manoah and his wife respond to the angel's departure.

The angel ascends in the flame of the altar offering. Manoah, watching, concludes they will die — *we have seen God*. His wife corrects him, calmly and with precision: if the LORD had intended to kill them, he would not have accepted a burnt offering from their hands, would not have shown them these things, and would not have announced a son. The logic is simple, structured, and correct. The woman who received the annunciation also provides the theological commentary on it. Her husband's response to divine encounter is terror and catastrophizing; hers is inference and assurance.

This scene is not incidental. It establishes the interpretive key for the chapters that follow: the woman in the Samson narrative will consistently see more clearly than the man. Manoah's wife perceives the angel's identity, reasons from evidence, and provides comfort. Samson will consistently fail to do any of these things — including, catastrophically, in the

Delilah narrative — and the contrast with his mother's clarity will make the failure sharper.

---

3. The Forbidden Desire and the Divine Utility

Samson goes to Timnah and sees a Philistine woman. He returns to his parents and announces that he wants to marry her. They object — is there no woman among your own people? But Samson is not asking. He instructs: *get her for me, for she is right in my eyes.*

Right in my eyes. This is the refrain of the book turned personal. The phrase used to diagnose the entire community's failure — everyone doing what was *right in their own eyes* — is now placed in Samson's mouth as his explicit rationale for the one thing most likely to undo his consecration: a Philistine wife who will serve as his handler before the chapter ends.

And then the narrator intervenes with the most theologically loaded parenthetical in the book:

"His father and mother did not know that it was from the LORD, for he was seeking an opportunity against the Philistines." — Judges 14:4

The forbidden desire was divinely directed. God was using Samson's pursuit of the prohibited to create a pretext for conflict with the Philistines. This does not mean Samson's behavior was endorsed or that the violation was erased. It means God was working through the trajectory Samson had already chosen — the same principle that operates across the entire Deuteronomistic history, and that produces some of its most uncomfortable theology. There is a difference between *God caused this* and *God used this.* The narrator uses language that deliberately blurs that line. The reader is meant to sit with the discomfort rather than resolve it.

4. The Lion, the Carcass, and the Honey

On the road to Timnah, the Spirit of the LORD rushes upon Samson and he tears a young lion apart with his bare hands, as one tears a young goat. He tells neither parent. He continues to the woman.

Later, returning to marry her, he turns aside to look at the lion's carcass. There is a swarm of bees inside it, and honey. He takes the honey with his hands and eats it on the road, giving some to his parents — but not telling them where it came from.

Two violations are layered here. The first is contact with the carcass — a direct violation of the Nazirite prohibition on touching the dead. The second is the concealment. He does not tell his parents where the honey came from. He carries the violation secretly, distributing its sweetness while hiding its source. The honey is real. The transgression producing it is also real. He has found a way to enjoy the fruit of his own boundary-crossing and pass it along as a gift, and no one who receives it knows what they are receiving.

This is the compressed image the entire Samson narrative will expand. Something deadly becomes the source of something sweet, but only through a violation that cannot be named openly. The honey from the lion is beautiful and prohibited simultaneously.

5. The Riddle and Its Betrayal

At the wedding feast — a seven-day celebration, consistent with Philistine custom and itself a question about how Samson is spending those seven days — he poses a riddle to his thirty companions:

"Out of the eater, something to eat; out of the strong, something sweet." — Judges 14:14

The stakes are material: thirty linen garments and thirty changes of clothing to the ones who solve it, or the same from them to Samson if they cannot. The companions cannot solve it in three days. On the fourth day they approach Samson's wife: *entice your husband to tell us the riddle, or we will burn you and your father's house with fire.*

The threat is not subtle. She is caught between a husband who poses riddles and Philistine men who issue ultimatums, and her husband's safety is not their concern. She weeps and presses Samson for the answer. He holds out for seven days — not because he is protecting a sacred secret, but because the riddle is built on a violation he has not confessed. Finally, he tells her. She tells the companions.

"If you had not plowed with my heifer, you would not have found out my riddle." — Judges 14:18

The insult is layered. She is his *heifer* — livestock, property, a working animal. His anger at her betrayal expresses itself as ownership language. He is furious that the tool he married has been used against him by other people, and his fury does not pause to consider why she was used or what it cost her.

The Spirit of the LORD rushes on him again. He goes to Ashkelon, kills thirty men, takes their spoil, and gives the garments to the riddle-solvers. He returns in anger to his father's house. His wife is given to his companion.

---

6. The Pattern Already Visible

By the end of chapter 14, the Samson narrative's structure is already complete. Everything that follows will be variation on what is already established here:

The Spirit empowers him. He pursues the forbidden. The forbidden produces conflict. The conflict produces violence. The violence produces a settlement that doesn't last. He moves to the next forbidden thing.

What the text does not give us is interiority. We do not know if Samson experiences his Nazirite vow as a constraint. We do not know if he feels the gap between who he was consecrated to be and who he is. He does not lament. He does not repent. He simply lives in the gap and keeps moving. The reader experiences the irony; the narrative offers no evidence that Samson does.

The man most completely consecrated — by a divine annunciation, before birth, with a lifetime Nazirite vow — becomes the book's longest portrait of consecration systematically undone from the inside. This is not accidental. The book of Judges has been building toward a question: what does calling look like when it is never matched by character? Samson is the full answer. His calling is total. His character is its own argument.

The Numbered Wrongs

- Samson's rationale for the Timnite marriage is explicitly that she is *right in my eyes* — the diagnostic phrase of the book's entire collapse, voiced here as personal justification for a prohibited union.

- He violates the Nazirite prohibition on contact with the dead by handling the lion's carcass and eating the honey from it. He does not acknowledge the violation, confess it, or seek any form of restoration.

- He distributes the honey to his parents without disclosing its source — concealing the transgression while sharing its benefit.

- When his wife gives away the riddle's answer under coercion and threat, his first response is a livestock insult: she is his *heifer*. The text shows no awareness that she was threatened with death, or that her position in this story is not a betrayal but a survival response.

- He kills thirty men at Ashkelon to pay a wager lost because of his wife's coercion. The thirty men at Ashkelon had no part in the riddle. Their deaths are the collateral cost of a private dispute.

- He returns to his father's house in anger and abandons his wife to the household. She is subsequently given to his companion. His abandonment creates the conditions for the next escalation.

Legal-Canonical Framework

Numbers 6:1–8 — The Nazirite law in full. The prohibitions are explicit: no grape product, no razor, no contact with the dead. Samson violates the prohibition on corpse contact in chapter 14 when he handles the lion carcass; he will violate the prohibition on wine at his wedding feast (the Hebrew *mišteh*, "feast," in 14:10 is the same word used for drinking parties); and the razor prohibition will be addressed by Delilah in chapter 16.

Numbers 6:9–12 — The defilement provision. If a Nazirite becomes defiled through accidental contact with the dead, there is a seven-day purification ritual, a sin offering, a burnt offering, and a restart of the dedication period. Samson accesses none of this. The violation is absorbed in silence.

Deuteronomy 7:3–4 — Neither shall you make marriages with them... for they will turn away your son from following me, that they may serve other gods.

The Timnite marriage is prohibited under this framework. The narrator acknowledges this and simultaneously attributes Samson's forbidden desire to divine orchestration — the most explicit statement in Judges that God operates through human violation without that violation becoming permissible.

Deuteronomy 6:18 — You shall do what is right and good in the sight of the LORD.

The contrast with Samson's *right in my eyes* is definitional. The legal framework consistently defines rightness as an external standard; Samson defines it as personal desire. This is the Judges refrain made individual and explicit.

New Testament Resonance

Hebrews 11:32 names Samson in the faith hall of fame alongside Gideon, Barak, and Jephthah. The same interpretive principle applies here as in the Jephthah chapter: Hebrews is acknowledging the faith-acts, not endorsing the character or the methods. The hall of fame includes Rahab, a prostitute; it includes Samson, who will spend the next two chapters compounding every failure established in these first two. The list is a gallery of the ones who — in some specific dimension — trusted God rather than what they could see. It is not a gallery of the morally exemplary. The company Samson keeps in Hebrews 11 is itself an argument about the kind of instrument God uses — which is both a word of grace and a warning against reading it as endorsement.

Romans 7:15, 19 — For what I do, I do not understand: for not what I would, that I do; but what I hate, that I do... For the good that I would, I do not: but the evil which I would not, that I do.

Paul is describing the structural condition of the person caught between law and desire, consecration and failure. Samson may be the Old Testament's most sustained narrative embodiment of this condition — with the added complication that the text offers no evidence he experiences it as conflict. He does not seem to hate what he does. He simply does it. The reader experiences the conflict that Samson himself may not.

1 Corinthians 1:27 — *God chose the foolish things of the world to shame the wise; God chose the weak things of the world to shame the strong.* The Samson narrative pushes on this from an uncomfortable angle: the instrument is not weak in the physical sense, but is profoundly weak in every other register. The strength is real. The failure is real. The two do not cancel each other out, and the reader is not permitted to use one to excuse the other.

92

Discussion Questions

1. The narrator tells us Samson's forbidden desire for the Timnite woman was *from the LORD* — God was seeking an opportunity through Samson's prohibited pursuit. How do you hold together divine sovereignty and human moral responsibility in a passage like this? Does the statement that God used Samson's failure reduce his responsibility for it? What does it do to your understanding of divine providence?

2. Samson's mother receives the annunciation directly, interprets the angel's departure correctly, and provides the theological correction when her husband catastrophizes. She is the most epistemically reliable figure in the birth narrative. What does the text accomplish by giving the consecrated man the most theologically clear-sighted mother — and then tracing what he does with the inheritance she represents?

3. Samson's rationale for the Timnite marriage is *she is right in my eyes* — the exact phrasing the book uses to diagnose the community's entire collapse. Was this phrasing intentional on Samson's part, or is it the narrator's signal to the reader? What is the difference? And what does it mean that the book's most consecrated figure uses the book's most diagnostic phrase to justify his first major decision?

4. He distributes the honey to his parents without telling them its source. The sweetness is real; the violation producing it is concealed. Where do you see this pattern operating — in communities of faith, in leadership, in personal spiritual life — the benefit of a transgression

made available to others while the transgression itself remains hidden?

5. When his wife gives away the riddle's answer, Samson calls her his *heifer*. She had been threatened with death. His response makes her position in the story entirely about what it cost him. How does the text's recording of this language — without editorial comment — function as indictment? What does the absence of commentary demand of the reader?

6. Samson is named in Hebrews 11 among those commended for faith. By the end of chapter 14, he has violated his Nazirite vow, insulted his wife, killed thirty men to pay a social debt, and abandoned the woman he married. What is the faith Hebrews is commending? And what does the canon's refusal to let that commendation erase the record of failure say about how Scripture holds together calling and character?

Chapter Ten: Micah's Shrine — Privatized Religion

Reference: Judges 17–18

The Story We Tell Children

A man named Micah made some idols and hired his own priest. Some Danite warriors came through, stole his idols and his priest, and set up their own shrine up north.

That's the version. It makes the story sound like a territorial dispute with a religious subplot. The text closes with one of the sharpest ironies in all of Scripture.

The Slower Reading

1. The Logic of Privatized Religion

Micah steals silver from his mother, confesses when she curses the thief — not knowing it was him — and she dedicates part of it to making an idol. To worship God. She calls on the name of the LORD while commissioning a graven image. The contradiction is presented without comment. The text is not making a theological argument here; it is observing a phenomenon: people who believe they are worshiping God while doing the opposite of what God commanded, and who feel completely justified.

Micah sets up a full private shrine — ephod, teraphim, household idols, his son as priest. When a wandering Levite arrives, Micah immediately offers him salary, clothing, and food to be his personal priest. His reasoning:

"Now I know that the LORD will do good to me, because I have a Levite as priest." — Judges 17:13

The sacred office has become a private service contract. God's favor is expected because the correct religious professional has been retained.

Two things are worth noting about how the text frames this. First, Micah is not worshiping a foreign god. He invokes the name of the LORD throughout. He is not an apostate in the simple sense. He has constructed a theological system in which personal devotion, private infrastructure, and professional clergy combine to produce divine favor — and he cannot see anything wrong with it. The problem is not that he has rejected God. The problem is that he has redefined what it means to be in right relationship with God in terms that center entirely on himself.

Second, the narrator does not interrupt the scene with an editorial correction. There is no "but this was evil in the sight of the LORD" appended to the chapter. The reader is expected to bring the legal framework — Deuteronomy, Leviticus, the prohibitions against graven images, the centralizing of worship, the regulation of the priesthood — and see what Micah cannot see: that the form of his religion has displaced its substance entirely.

2. The Danites and Institutional Theft

The tribe of Dan is still landless. Their territorial allotment from Joshua has not been secured. Five spies, scouting for somewhere the tribe can settle, pass through the hill country of Ephraim and encounter Micah's Levite. They recognize the voice and ask him to inquire of God about their mission. He does. He assures them the journey will succeed.

When the five return with six hundred Danite warriors, they stop at Micah's house on the way through. The five spies know what is in the shrine. While the warriors stand at the gate, the five men take the idols, the ephod, and the teraphim. The Levite objects — mildly. The Danites' response is immediate and practical: come with us and be priest to a tribe rather than just to a household.

"And the priest's heart was glad. He took the ephod and the household gods and the carved image and went along with the people." — Judges 18:20

The hesitation is resolved by the larger opportunity. The Levite's initial attachment to Micah was never a matter of vocation or loyalty. It was a job. When a better offer came, he took it. Micah's protest when he finds his shrine empty is the text's most darkly comic moment:

"You have taken my gods that I made and the priest, and you have gone away, and what have I left?" — Judges 18:24

My gods that I made. The man who began the story by invoking the name of the LORD has arrived at a theology in which he manufactures his own gods and experiences their theft as personal loss. The progression is not sudden. It is the logical endpoint of the system he constructed from the beginning: a religion centered on himself, built with his own hands, staffed by a professional he retained, now stripped bare because someone with more power wanted it.

The Danites conquer the peaceful city of Laish — a city, the narrator emphasizes, whose people were quiet and unsuspecting, with no one to deliver them. They rename it Dan and establish the shrine there. The narrator records that the shrine persisted *"until the day of the captivity of the land"* (18:30). This is not a brief aberration. It is the founding of a lasting institution.

3. The Identity Reveal

The Levite's name has been withheld through the entire narrative. The reader knows him only as a wandering Levite from Bethlehem, a man without position who found one through a private service contract and upgraded it when the opportunity arose.

The final verse of chapter 18 provides the name:

"And Jonathan the son of Gershom, son of Moses, and his sons were priests to the tribe of Dan until the day of the captivity of the land." — Judges 18:30

Jonathan. Son of Gershom. Son of Moses.

The idolatrous shrine at Dan is served by a grandson of the lawgiver. Moses' descendant is the priest of the shrine that worships what Moses' law prohibits. The man whose grandfather stood on Sinai and received the commandment against graven images is the professional clergy for the graven image made from stolen silver.

The genealogy cannot be accidental. The author knew this detail throughout. The author chose to withhold it until the last possible moment. The irony is structural: the most complete violation of the covenant is being serviced by the most direct descendant of the covenant's mediator. It is not enough that Israel has abandoned the law. The law's own lineage has been absorbed into the apparatus of its abandonment.

This is where the chapter ends — not with a prophet's rebuke, not with divine judgment, not with any restoration. It ends with a name and a duration. The shrine was there. Jonathan served it. And it lasted.

Legal-Canonical Framework

Exodus 20:3–5 — You shall have no other gods before me. You shall not make for yourself any graven image.

The first and second commandments. Micah's mother commissions the idol while blessing the thief in the name of the LORD. The invocation of the covenant name alongside the manufacture of a prohibited object is not incidental — it is precisely the confusion these commandments were designed to prevent.

Deuteronomy 12:2–5, 13–14 — The centralization command: Israel is not to offer worship wherever they choose but only in the place the LORD will designate. Every element of Micah's shrine violates this framework. So does the Danite shrine at Dan. Both are private religious establishments operating outside the covenant's provisions for how worship is to be conducted and where.

Numbers 3:5–10; 18:1–7 — The regulation of the priesthood. Levitical service is not freelance. The tribe of Levi is set apart for specific functions within the covenant community's cultic life, operating under defined structures. The wandering Levite's willingness to serve as a household priest for wages — and then to upgrade to a tribal shrine — reflects the collapse of the institutional structures that were supposed to govern his vocation.

Deuteronomy 17:8–13 — Disputes involving law and religious matters are to be brought before the priests and judges at the designated place. Micah's Levite dispenses oracular guidance from a private shrine for private pay. The judicial and oracular functions of the Levitical priesthood have been privatized.

1 Kings 12:28–30 — Jeroboam, after the kingdom splits, establishes two golden calves — one at Bethel, one at Dan — and says: *"Here are your gods, O Israel, who brought you up out of Egypt."* The shrine Judges describes at Dan is the precursor to the shrine Jeroboam will establish there. The narrator's note that the Danite shrine lasted *"until the captivity of the land"* connects directly to the Northern Kingdom's fall. An act of religious privatization in the period of the judges becomes the founding infrastructure of the Northern Kingdom's state idolatry. The trajectory runs from Micah's household silver to the golden calves that define Israel's apostasy for the rest of the Deuteronomistic history.

Matthew 15:1–9 / Mark 7:6–8 — Jesus quotes Isaiah against the Pharisees: *"This people honors me with their lips, but their heart is far from me; in vain do they worship me, teaching as doctrines the commandments of men."* Micah's shrine illustrates this dynamic in its oldest form: religious practice meticulously maintained, religious professionals properly retained, religious language consistently employed — and the entire apparatus serving a center other than God.

2 Timothy 4:3–4 — *"For the time is coming when people will not endure sound teaching, but having itching ears they will accumulate for themselves teachers to suit their own passions."* The Levite who moves from household shrine to tribal shrine when a better offer arrives is the teacher who follows the market. The dynamic Paul warns about is already present in the Danite priest: the religious professional whose loyalty is to the congregation with the best terms.

Acts 8:18–24 — Simon Magus attempts to purchase the power of the Spirit with money. Peter's rebuke names the error: *"You have neither part nor lot in this matter, for your heart is not right before God."* Micah's expectation that retaining a Levite guarantees divine favor is the same error — the sacred reduced to a commodity, God's presence made available through correct professional procurement.

1 Corinthians 3:16–17 — *"Do you not know that you are God's temple and that God's Spirit dwells in you? If anyone destroys God's temple, God will destroy him."* Paul's argument assumes a community that cannot be organized around private, self-constructed versions of access to God. The contrast with Micah's shrine is structural: the temple is not a private installation but a community of persons in whom the

Spirit dwells. You cannot hire your way into it or steal your way out with the furniture.

Discussion Questions

1. Micah's mother invokes the name of the LORD while commissioning an idol. Micah expects divine blessing because he has retained the correct religious professional. Both are using the language and forms of genuine religion to construct something that serves their own purposes. What is the difference between religious form and actual faithfulness? What does it look like when communities confuse the maintenance of religious structures with the actual presence of God — and how would you know if you were doing it?

2. The Levite accepts Micah's offer with minimal hesitation and then accepts the Danites' larger offer with less. The sacred office becomes a career trajectory. Where do you see similar dynamics in contemporary religious life — ministry as professional advancement, vocation as brand, the priesthood of a calling reduced to the terms of a contract? What does the Levite's ease of movement say about what he actually believed about his vocation?

3. Micah says *"my gods that I made."* He began the chapter invoking the LORD and ends it speaking of gods he manufactured. The text does not mark this as a dramatic fall — it presents it as the natural conclusion of the system he built from the beginning. What is the mechanism by which sincere religious devotion becomes self-referential religion? What are the early markers, and why are they so hard to see from the inside?

4. Jonathan, grandson of Moses, is the priest of the idolatrous shrine. What does this say about the

relationship between lineage, formation, and faithfulness? Does proximity to greatness — a grandfather who stood on Sinai, a family that carried the law — guarantee anything? Where in the narrative might we locate the failure of transmission? And what does it demand of communities who have inherited something worth transmitting?

5. The narrator tells us the shrine lasted *"until the day of the captivity of the land."* It was not corrected. It was not shut down. It persisted and became the model for Jeroboam's state religion. What does it mean that a private act of religious self-construction became a lasting institution — and that the institution outlasted the corrective structures that should have addressed it? What does this suggest about the staying power of religious error once it is institutionalized?

6. The chapter ends with a name and a duration — no judgment, no restoration, no prophet, no divine word. The narrator simply tells us what happened and how long it lasted. What is the effect of that silence? What is the reader meant to do with a chapter that ends without resolution?

Chapter Eleven: The Concubine of Gibeah — The Story Israel Told Wrong

Reference: Judges 19–21

The Story We Tell Children

A terrible crime happened in the city of Gibeah. The men of Benjamin wouldn't listen to justice, so the other tribes had to go to war against them. Benjamin was almost wiped out, but in the end Israel found a way to preserve the tribe.

That's the version. It makes the story sound like a painful but ultimately resolved legal crisis — a matter of tribal governance with a tragic body count. The text is doing something far more devastating: it is presenting the complete moral collapse of the covenant community, and placing a nameless woman's death at the center of it.

The Slower Reading

1. The Deliberate Echo of Genesis 19

Before a word can be said about the concubine, the reader must see what the narrator is doing structurally.

Judges 19 is a rewrite of Genesis 19. The parallels are not accidental — they are the argument. A traveler arrives in a city. He sits in the public square without a host. An old man takes him in. Men of the city surround the house after dark and beat on the door. Their demand is word for word the demand of the Sodom mob: bring out the man who came into your house, that we may know him. The host offers a woman instead. Violence happens outside. The traveler departs in the morning.

In Genesis 19, the city is Sodom — proverbially wicked, Canaanite, judged and destroyed by God. In Judges 19, the city is Gibeah — an Israelite city, belonging to the tribe of Benjamin. The Levite chose to bypass Jebus — the foreign city, the future Jerusalem — because he did not want to lodge among strangers. He passed the Canaanite city to find safety among his own people. He found Sodom.

This is the book's thesis, stated in narrative form: Israel has become what it was supposed to displace. The conquest was incomplete. The cycle completed. The appendices are showing what it produced. When the narrator mirrors Sodom onto an Israelite city, the reader is meant to feel the full weight of what has happened to the covenant community by chapter nineteen.

"As they were making their hearts merry, behold, the men of the city, worthless fellows, surrounded the house, beating on

the door. And they said to the old man, 'Bring out the man who came into your house, that we may know him.'" — Judges 19:22

2. The Concubine — Who Has No Name

She is called the Levite's *pilegesh* — his concubine. She is given no name. She will not receive one at any point in chapters 19, 20, or 21. The reader will follow her from Bethlehem to Gibeah to a doorstep at dawn, and will never know what she was called.

The chapter begins with her departure. She left the Levite — the Hebrew says she *played the harlot against him*, though the Septuagint reads she *was angry with him*. The textual variant is significant: the difference between a woman who committed infidelity and a woman who was angry enough to leave is not trivial, and the narrator does not resolve it. She returns to her father's house in Bethlehem. Her father's hospitality to the Levite when he comes to retrieve her is extensive — five days of eating, drinking, and delay. The concubine does not speak during this visit. She is the occasion of the reunion. She is not a participant in it.

On the road home, they stop in Gibeah of Benjamin rather than Jebus. The choice is the Levite's. No one takes them in until an old man from the hill country of Ephraim — himself a resident alien in Gibeah — offers his house.

What happens next requires the reader to stay close to the text and not look away.

The men of Gibeah surround the house and demand the Levite. The host offers his daughter and the concubine. The men are not interested. And then — *"But the man seized his concubine and put her out to them. And they knew her and abused her all night until the morning."* (Judges 19:25)

The Levite threw her out the door.

This is not ambiguous. The verb is *wayya ḥazēq* — he seized, he grabbed. He took his concubine and he put her outside. The text records his agency clearly. He made the decision. Her body absorbed the violence directed at his.

She was raped and abused from nightfall to dawn. In the morning she returned to the house — fell at the door, hands on the threshold — and was found there by the Levite when he rose to continue his journey.

"When her master got up in the morning and opened the door of the house to continue on his way, there lay his concubine, fallen in the doorway with her hands on the threshold. He said to her, 'Get up, let's go.' But there was no answer." — Judges 19:27–28

She does not answer because she is dead.

The Levite places her body on the donkey and travels home. The text does not tell us whether he checked for a pulse. It does not record grief. It records logistics.

3. The Levite's Culpability

The Levite's behavior from beginning to end is a study in progressive failure of care that the text records without naming.

He arrives in Bethlehem to retrieve the concubine who left him and spends five days in comfortable hospitality with her father, feasting and drinking. She remains silent. He delays. His urgency to reclaim her does not manifest as any particular attention to her. When the old man offers his daughter and the concubine to the mob, the Levite does not protest. He seizes her and sends her out. When she is found at dawn, his words are the words of a man addressing a sleeping servant: *Get up, let's go.* There is no pause recorded. No check. No acknowledgment.

He then cuts her body into twelve pieces — an act that instrumentalizes her death into a political message — and sends one to each tribe of Israel.

When the assembly gathers at Mizpah and he tells his story, the retelling must be read against what the narrator recorded in chapter nineteen. In his account, the men of Gibeah *came after him*, intending to kill *him*. He is the center of his own victimization. *They raped my concubine, and she died.* The passive construction erases his agency entirely. The man who seized her and put her outside does not appear in his own testimony. He was the victim. They were the perpetrators. She was what happened in between.

The assembly mobilizes on the basis of his account. A civil war begins. The concubine is never named. No one asks the Levite why he opened the door.

The word the Levite uses for what was done to her — *vaye'annu* — is the same root as *anah*, the word the Torah uses for Israel's oppression in Egypt, the word used for what Sarah did to Hagar. The vocabulary of slavery and affliction. The text uses the language of Egypt to describe what the Levite did to his own household. The narrator is not subtle about this. The reader is meant to recognize the echo.

4. Her Hands on the Threshold

There is a detail in this narrative that will not be managed.

She came back.

After a night of gang rape, with whatever was left, she crawled back to the door of the house where her master had been sleeping and put her hands on the threshold. The text records the position of her hands. We do not know if she was trying to get in. We do not know if she called out. We do not know whether she was alive when the Levite opened the door or whether she had died in the night. The text does not tell us. The Levite does not ask.

What the text gives us is her return. The theological weight of that detail belongs to her. It cannot be transferred to the Levite's grief or the assembly's outrage or the civil war that follows. A nameless woman who was used, discarded, and destroyed came back to the door. The book of Judges, which has been cataloguing Israel's failure for nineteen chapters, reserves its most arresting image for her: hands on the threshold, facing toward the house.

Phyllis Trible, in *Texts of Terror*, names her a victim in a text that does not give her the dignity of a name — and argues, correctly, that the chapter's job is to be the advocate the text itself demands. Not by importing external frameworks onto the narrative, but by reading the Torah's own categories against what happens in it. Leviticus 19:16 — *You shall not stand against the blood of your neighbor.* — is violated by every person in this chapter. The old man's hospitality extends to the Levite and not to the concubine. The Levite's self-preservation extends to himself and not to her. The assembly's justice extends to the crime against the Levite and not to the crime committed by the Levite.

She is the story. The civil war, the tribal politics, the near-extinction of Benjamin — these are what the narrative generates. She is what the narrative is about.

5. Her Namelessness

She is never named.

The text names the Ammonite king in Jephthah's chapter. It names the cities Jephthah punishes. It names the Ephraimite soldiers tested at the ford. In the Gibeah narrative, it names the old man's city of origin. It does not name the concubine. Like Jephthah's daughter before her — another woman who moves through a consequential narrative without a name — she is identified entirely by her relationship to a man.

This is not an accident of incomplete records. Names are withheld deliberately in biblical narrative. The narrator who remembered that Jonathan was Moses' grandson and withheld that detail until the last verse of chapter 18 is a narrator who exercises full control over the disclosure of names. The concubine's namelessness is a choice. It is a literary and theological signal: this is what the community did not feel. That she mattered. That she was a person with a name. The namelessness is an indictment built into the grammar of the text.

The reader who knows her name is no one. The reader who feels the weight of not knowing it is exactly where the narrator intends them to be.

6. The Solution That Compounds the Violence

Israel's response to the crime is civil war against Benjamin — which the text frames as appropriate. But the war nearly annihilates the tribe. After two disastrous initial defeats, Israel breaks Benjamin: six hundred men flee to the rock of Rimmon; twenty-five thousand Benjaminites are dead.

Then follows the problem: the assembly had sworn not to give daughters to Benjamin. A tribe of Israel is nearly extinct.

The solution the assembly constructs is worth reading without flinching.

First, they discover that no one from Jabesh-gilead came to the assembly. They send twelve thousand warriors to massacre the city — every man, every married woman — and bring back the four hundred virgins they find. This is authorized by the assembly. These four hundred women are given to the surviving Benjaminites.

Still short. The solution for the remaining two hundred: the assembly gives the Benjaminites permission to abduct daughters of Shiloh from the annual festival. Not to marry them with the fathers' consent — to take them. *"So go and lie in ambush in the vineyards and watch. If the daughters of Shiloh come out to dance in the dances, then come out of the vineyards and snatch each man his wife from the daughters of Shiloh."* (Judges 21:20–21)

The community that gathered to avenge a sexual crime solves its downstream problem by commissioning further sexual crimes. The assembly that wept and asked God why this catastrophe had come upon Israel authorized the abduction of young women as a bureaucratic fix. The moral logic has not simply failed — it has inverted. The community is now doing structurally what it went to war to punish.

The concubine began the narrative as one woman without a name. She ends it as the origin point of a catastrophe that leaves hundreds of women without names, without choices, distributed among survivors as solutions to a problem no one will acknowledge creating.

"In those days there was no king in Israel. Everyone did what was right in their own eyes." — Judges 21:25

The book ends here.

114

Legal-Canonical Framework

Leviticus 19:16 — *Do not stand idly by when your neighbor's life is at stake.* Every male in the narrative violates this. The old man, the Levite, and ultimately the assembly that mobilizes to avenge the Levite without inquiring into his role. The concubine's life is at stake. No one stands.

Exodus 22:21–22; Deuteronomy 10:18–19 — The Torah's consistent protection of the widow, the orphan, and the vulnerable within the covenant community. She is a concubine — marginalized in status, dependent for protection on the man who sent her outside. The categories of vulnerability the Torah names as deserving protection describe her precisely. The community's failure to protect her is not incidental. It is a failure of the covenant's most basic social obligations.

Deuteronomy 22:25–27 — But if a man finds a betrothed damsel in the field, and the man force her... then the man only that lay with her shall die... for he found her in the field, and the betrothed damsel cried, and there was none to save her.

The law assumes the obligation to save. The Levite was in the house. There was someone who could have saved her. The law's assumption is the indictment.

Genesis 19 — The deliberate Sodom parallel, discussed above. The reader who comes to Judges 19 already knowing what happened in Genesis 19 is being asked a specific question: if Sodom was destroyed for this, what does it mean that Israel has become Sodom? The answer the book provides is the rest of the canon: the monarchy, the prophets, the exile. The trajectory from Gibeah runs forward.

Deuteronomy 17:14–20 — The law of the king. The closing refrain of Judges — *in those days there was no king in Israel*

— points forward to this legal provision. But the Deuteronomistic history will make clear that monarchy does not solve what is wrong with Israel. Saul, David, Solomon — the kings do what is right in their own eyes just as thoroughly as the judges. The refrain is not a solution. It is a diagnosis pointing at a solution that will itself require further diagnosis.

New Testament Resonance

The concubine of Gibeah has no New Testament referent. The New Testament does not quote Judges 19. No epistle returns to it. No Gospel invokes it.

This absence is itself worth naming. The story that ended the book of Judges — the most disturbing narrative in the Hebrew Bible's historical literature — is not resolved in the canon by a later text that provides comfort or redemption or closure. The reader must sit with what Judges 19–21 produces without the relief of a New Testament passage that wraps it.

What the New Testament does provide are the categories.

Matthew 25:31–46 — The sheep and the goats are divided by their response to the vulnerable: the hungry, the stranger, the naked, the prisoner. Inasmuch as you did it not to one of the least of these, you did it not to me.

The concubine of Gibeah is the least of these. No one fed her. No one welcomed her. No one clothed her. The Levite said *get up* to a dead woman. The categories of Matthew 25 are not new. They are the categories of Leviticus 19 applied to human faces. Judges 19 shows what happens when an entire community fails to apply them.

Luke 18:1–8 — The parable of the persistent widow, who cried out to an unjust judge and at last received justice because of her continual coming. Jesus frames this parable around the question: *will God not give justice to his elect who cry out to him day and night?* The implication is that God hears. The concubine's hands were on the threshold. She came back. There is no parable in the text to assure the reader that she was heard. The reader must bring to the text what the text does not provide — the conviction that someone, somewhere in the canon, sees what the Levite would not. The New Testament's answer is yes. But it does not name her.

Romans 12:19 — *Beloved, never avenge yourselves, but leave it to the wrath of God, for it is written, "Vengeance is mine, I will repay, says the Lord."* The civil war triggered by the Levite's testimony is not divine vengeance. It is the assembly's vengeance, misframed as justice, executed without full information, and generating further violence in its wake. The canon's answer to the violence of Judges 19–21 is not more violence. Paul, quoting Deuteronomy, points to a different register entirely.

Revelation 6:9–10 — The souls under the altar cry out: How long, O Lord, holy and true, do you not judge and avenge our blood on them that dwell on the earth?

The nameless concubine does not appear in this vision by name. The category includes her. The New Testament's final answer to the question of what happens to the unnamed, unavenged victims of the covenant community's failures is eschatological: *a little longer*. This is not comfort designed to minimize the crime. It is the assurance that the accounting has not been forgotten. The hands on the threshold are in the record of the one who does not stand idly by.

Discussion Questions

1. The narrator deliberately mirrors Judges 19 on Genesis 19, placing the Sodom narrative onto an Israelite city. What is the theological weight of that comparison? What does it mean that the traveler bypassed the Canaanite city to find safety among his own people — and found Sodom? What does that demand of communities who identify themselves by their covenant distinctiveness?

2. The Levite's retelling to the assembly centers himself as the victim and erases his own action from the narrative. He is not lying about the crime — he is editing his role in it. Where do you see this pattern in communities responding to institutional failure: the acknowledgment of the crime alongside the erasure of complicity? What makes that form of testimony so persistent, and so damaging?

3. She came back. With whatever was left, she returned to the door and put her hands on the threshold. The text gives this detail without commentary. What do you do with it theologically? What does it mean that the narrative's most morally clear moment belongs to the person with no voice and no name?

4. The assembly's solution to the near-extinction of Benjamin required the massacre of Jabesh-gilead and the authorized abduction of the daughters of Shiloh. The community that gathered to avenge a sexual crime ends by commissioning further sexual crimes. What is the mechanism by which communities pursuing justice compound the injustice they set out to address? What

would repentance — as opposed to response — have looked like here?

5. The New Testament does not return to the concubine of Gibeah. There is no passage that resolves her story or promises her vindication by name. What does it mean to hold a text like this within a canon that claims God hears those who cry out — when the text itself gives no evidence that anyone heard? How does the reader navigate the gap between the canon's claims and the narrative's silence?

6. The book of Judges ends without restoration. No judge finally gets it right. No repentance produces lasting change. The last word is a refrain that functions as diagnosis. What does it mean to read a book of Scripture that ends in failure — and to recognize that the community that produced and preserved this text was willing to tell this story about itself? What does that willingness demand of readers who inherit the same tradition?

Author's note: This chapter requires the author to resist every interpretive pressure to make the concubine's story about something else — the tribal politics, the civil war, the question of monarchy, the problem of Benjamin. She is not a subplot. She is the subject. The chapter's task is to be the advocate the text demands, using the Torah's own framework to name what happened and why the community's failure to protect her is not incidental to the book's argument but its culmination. The reader who reaches the end of Judges should feel the weight of twenty-one chapters arriving at two hands on a threshold.

Epilogue: What the Book of Judges Is Not For

The Problem of the Precedent Reader

There is a mode of biblical reading that treats the narrative as a behavior catalog. If a person in the text did something and was not immediately struck down, the argument goes, then that thing must be permissible — or at least not seriously prohibited. This reading style has a long history, it shows up in serious theological debates, and it is the wrong tool for almost every book in the Hebrew Bible.

It is the wrong tool for Judges.

The book of Judges does not end with an unnamed woman's hands on a threshold in order to suggest that what happened to her was acceptable. It ends there because the narrator wanted the reader to feel the weight of twenty-one chapters arriving at a single image. Not a battle won, not a covenant renewed, not a prayer answered. Two hands. A threshold. The dark.

The community that produced and preserved this text was willing to tell this story about itself. That willingness is itself a theological act. It is not an endorsement of the behavior it describes.

The Difference Between Description and Prescription

Judges is a descriptive book. It describes what a community does when it operates without a framework beyond its own judgment. It describes what happens when the incomplete obedience of the prologue — the failure to displace, the tolerance of accommodation, the comfort with what was supposed to be temporary — is allowed to compound across generations.

Description is not prescription.

The text describes Jephthah making a rash vow. It does not prescribe human vows of that kind — the Torah's framework for vows, which Jephthah clearly violated, exists precisely because the narrative already demonstrated what happens without it. The text describes Gideon building an ephod. It does not prescribe private cult objects. The text describes Samson pursuing Philistine women in violation of his Nazirite consecration. It does not prescribe the pattern. In each case, the legal-canonical framework surrounding the narrative identifies the behavior as a violation and shows what it costs. The cost is the point.

Reading these narratives as permission rather than as warning requires ignoring the legal architecture the text was written inside — the same architecture this volume has been reading each chapter against. The Torah does not bracket itself when the narrative gets difficult. It applies.

The Benjamin Question

But Judges moves beyond private moral failure. The book's final chapters do not describe individuals making poor choices. They describe a community destroying one of its own constituent tribes. The near-annihilation of Benjamin — and the methods by which the remaining six hundred men were provided with wives — is not a story about sin with personal consequences. It is a story about institutionalized violence operated through the machinery of communal justice.

The assembly that gathered at Mizpah to address the crime at Gibeah was not wrong to gather. The crime demanded a response. What the text shows is how a community pursuing legitimate justice can, through the logic of its own momentum, compound the injustice it set out to address. The sworn oath not to give daughters to Benjamin was presumably made with some motivation the text does not record sympathetically enough to preserve. What the text does preserve is the outcome: the assembly that vowed to punish sexual violence solved the downstream problem it created by authorizing further sexual violence, on a larger scale, distributed bureaucratically across two additional populations of women.

This is not a model for anything. It is a diagnosis of what happens when a community pursues justice without repentance — when the appropriate response to a crime is mobilized through mechanisms that have themselves been corrupted by the same moral failure they are trying to address.

The tribe of Benjamin was nearly destroyed. The women of Jabesh-gilead were killed to provide four hundred wives for survivors. The daughters of Shiloh were abducted from a festival. The text records these events with the same flat precision it has used throughout the book for mounting catastrophe. There is no divine word ordering the massacre of Jabesh-gilead. There is no prophetic voice objecting to the abductions at Shiloh. There is only the assembly doing what it has decided to do, and the refrain that follows: *In those days there was no king in Israel. Everyone did what was right in their own eyes.*

The refrain is not ironic praise of the assembly's creativity. It is the book's final diagnosis of why any of this happened.

What the Refrain Actually Says

The phrase appears four times in the appendix section of Judges (17:6, 18:1, 19:1, 21:25). It has been read in two ways.

The first reading hears it as a pro-monarchy argument: what Israel needed was a king, and once it had one, these problems would resolve. This reading is not entirely wrong — the book is pointing toward Samuel and the monarchy. But it is incomplete. The monarchy that follows in Samuel and Kings will generate its own catastrophe, in some cases worse. The books of Samuel and Kings are not a correction of Judges. They are its sequel — the same human pattern operating at a different institutional scale. Kings fall into the same cycle as judges, with more resources and more people to damage in the collapse.

The second reading, and the more accurate one, hears the refrain as a covenant argument. The issue is not the absence of a king. The issue is the absence of any authority structure capable of binding the community to something beyond its own preferences. A king could provide that structure — or could fail to, as most of the subsequent kings will. The refrain is not a promise that monarchy will fix things. It is a description of what happens when a community has no center of gravity beyond collective self-interest.

In those days there was no king in Israel. No authority the community recognized as binding. No covenant framework it was willing to hold itself to. Everyone did what was right in their own eyes — which is to say, everyone applied their own judgment as the final criterion, and the cumulative result of all that sovereign individual and collective judgment was an unnamed woman's hands on a threshold.

The Hermeneutical Warning

There are communities that read Judges and come away with arguments for polygamy, for holy war, for the subordination of women, for tribal exclusivism, for vengeance theology. This reading requires treating the text as a permission slip for whatever behaviors one has decided in advance to endorse, and filtering out everything the text says about the consequences of those behaviors.

The same text that describes Gideon's many wives also shows his son Abimelech murdering sixty-nine brothers. The connection is not incidental. The text is drawing it explicitly.

The same text that describes the assembly's military campaign against Benjamin also shows the assembly authorizing the abduction of the daughters of Shiloh as a bureaucratic fix. The connection is not incidental. The text is drawing it explicitly.

Judges is a book about the logic of accommodation. Small failures of obedience — the Canaanite cities left in place, the incomplete displacement, the temporary compromises — compound across generations into the thing they were designed to prevent. The community that was supposed to model a different way of ordering life under covenant becomes, chapter by chapter, the thing it was told to displace. By the final chapter, an Israelite city is enacting the Sodom narrative. The reader who remembered Genesis 19 when reading Judges 19 was supposed to feel that.

The book does not offer a solution. It offers an accurate diagnosis. The diagnosis is this: a community that treats the framework designed to protect the vulnerable as optional, that accommodates what it was told to displace, that cycles through remorse without changing its behavior, will eventually become what it was supposed to oppose. The violence will not stay contained in individual acts. It will become institutional. It will be authorized by the assembly. It will be operated through the mechanisms of communal justice. And the last people it will protect are the ones who most needed protection.

What Follows

The reader who closes Judges and opens Ruth finds a story of loyalty and redemption that operates in the same period — "in the days when the judges ruled" (Ruth 1:1). It is not an accident that the canon places Ruth immediately after Judges. The contrast is deliberate. Ruth is a foreign woman who chooses covenant faithfulness with more consistency than most of the Israelites in the preceding twenty-one chapters. Boaz is a man who operates within the legal framework of his community in a way none of the judges managed for long. The redemption the book describes is not spectacular. It is quiet, careful, legal, and personal.

The book of Judges ends in catastrophe. The book of Ruth, which shares its era, ends with a genealogy leading to David. The canon is making an argument about where genuine covenant faithfulness is found — not in the military deliverer whose Spirit-empowered victories mask private moral collapse, but in the widow who clung to her mother-in-law in a foreign country, and the man who noticed her at the edge of his field.

Judges is not a model. It is a mirror. The community that produced it was honest enough to record its own collapse, systematically and without excusing the figures at the center. That honesty is a form of faithfulness. It preserved the record not because the record was flattering, but because accurate diagnosis is the precondition for any genuine repentance.

The reader who reaches the end of Judges having felt the weight of it — having followed the descending arc from Othniel's uncomplicated obedience to the unnamed woman's hands on the threshold — is in exactly the position the narrator intended. Not comfortable. Not equipped with permission for behavior the text has been identifying as catastrophic. Prepared, instead, to read Samuel with a clear understanding of what the monarchy was inheriting, and why the solution would be harder than anyone hoped.

The book ends. The woman is still nameless. The refrain is still a diagnosis. The hands are still on the threshold. That is where the narrator left us, and it is the right place to end.

Discussion Questions

1. The precedent-reader argument — "they did this in the Bible and didn't go to hell for it" — is a hermeneutical claim about how Scripture authorizes behavior. What are the conditions under which that argument would be valid, and where does it break down? What does it require the reader to ignore in order to function?

2. The community at the end of Judges pursues justice through mechanisms that have been corrupted by the same failure they are trying to address. What does repentance — as opposed to response — look like for a community in that position? What would it have required of the assembly at Mizpah that the text shows them unwilling to do?

3. The canon places Ruth immediately after Judges, set in the same era, demonstrating covenant faithfulness operating quietly in the space between catastrophes. What does that placement suggest about where the text expects genuine faithfulness to be found? Does it change how you read either book?

4. The book of Judges was preserved by the community that appears in it as the subject of a sustained indictment. What does that preservation tell us about the community's relationship to its own tradition? What does it demand of readers who inherit the same tradition?

5. The refrain — "everyone did what was right in their own eyes" — functions as diagnosis of a community with no binding center of gravity beyond collective preference. Where do you see that pattern operative today, and what does Judges suggest about where it leads? What would it take for a community to recognize that pattern in itself before the end of the book arrives?